PROFESSIONAL MALPRACTICE

by

Irving J. Sloan

Law for the Layperson

Oceana's Legal Almanacs, Second Series

Oceana Publications, Inc.

Dobbs Ferry, NY

Professional Malpractice. Sloan, Irving. 176 pages

ISBN: 0-379-111748
ISSN: 1059-5376

Printed in the United States on acid free paper.

TABLE OF CONTENTS

CHAPTER 1   PROFESSIONAL CONDUCT 1

CHAPTER 2   PHYSICIAN'S DUTIES TO
PATIENTS 7

CHAPTER 3   PHYSICIAN'S-PATIENT
RELATIONSHIP 21

CHAPTER 4   ELEMENTS OF
MALPRACTICE 31

CHAPTER 5   PERFORMANCE GROUNDS ... 45

CHAPTER 6   MALPRACTICE DEFENSES 55

CHAPTER 7   SCREENING PANELS AND
ARBITRATION 59

CHAPTER 8   ATTORNEY MALPRACTICE ... 65

CHAPTER 9   "OTHER" PROFESSIONS 77

APPENDIX A

APPENDIX B

APPENDIX C

PROFESSIONAL MALPRACTICE

CHAPTER 1

The Idea of a "Profession" and Professional Conduct

While the thrust and the bulk of this Legal Almanac volume deals with the legal malpractice issues which arise in the professional practices in medicine and law, especially medical malpractice, it is the author's essential purpose to bring to his readers' attention the broader topic of professional malpractice as related to the professions in general. As we shall see in this survey, a number of other professions are discussed, albeit in shorter chapters. For the most part, there are largely similar issues and theories which run through malpractice issues regardless of the professional task: We are dealing with negligence issues as they are applied to professional duties of care.

It does seem appropriate, therefore, to offer at the outset a broad view of what we mean when we speak about "the profession" and "professionals" that are by now a hallmark of modern post-industrial society. The law has increasingly intruded into professional autonomy. Not that rules of liability have not long played a major part in regulating the activities of the professions. The status of professionals attracted liability, from the time when veterinary surgeons in the 13th and 14th centuries were liable for their faulty work. The extraordinary power of professionals over clients brought about fiduciary obligations. The courts have implied terms in professionals' contracts that their services will be

1

performed to a competent level. And when the services of professional have resulted in physical harm to others, liability has been found under negligence, regardless of contract principles.

The recognition of the power of professions, and not only the well-known professions of law and medicine, but extending further to educators, clergymen, accountants, dentists *et al.,* has accelerated legal consequences for harm to patients and clients which could or should have been avoided.

First, at least one definition of "the professions". There is no unanimous agreement among the sociologists from whom legal writers take their cue. Talcott Parsons, long one of the country's leading sociologists, has noted that, "the boundaries of the group system we generally call the professions are fluid and indistinct. There are many borderline groups whose professional status is, for one reason or another, equivocal."[1]

First among these criteria is the requirement of formal technical training accompanied by some institutional mode of validating both the adequacy of the training and the competence of trained individuals. Among other things, the training must lead to some order of mastery of a generalized cultural tradition, and do so in a manner giving prominence to an intellectual

---

1   Parsons, "Professions" (1968) 3 *International Encyclopedia of Social Sciences* 536. He does, however, suggest some fundamental criteria:

component—that is, it must give primacy to the valuation of cognitive rationality as applied to a particular field. The second criterion is that not only must the cultural tradition be mastered, in the same sense of being understood, but skills in some form of its use must also be developed. The third core criterion is that a full-fledged profession must have some institutional means of making sure that such competence will be put to socially responsible uses.[2]

In plainer language, what we are talking about here is professional services (i.e., providing information and advice.) This involves (1) the application of skill to the performance of a task or the rendering of advice; the skill springs from a body of knowledge accumulated by intellectual effort that is the product of formal training, and (2) the performance of the tasks or the rendering of the advice is accompanied by ethical undertakings usually articulated by a representative body of practitioners.[3]

It is interesting and probably useful to relate here that when forced to a definition of "professional" in a law introduced into Congress to place a moratorium on the activity of the Federal trade Commission with respect to certain professions and

2   *Ibid.*
3   See, David F. Partlett, *Professional Negligence,* Law Book Company Ltd. (1985)

professional activities back in 1982, this aspect of professionalism was relied upon.

(3) The term "professional" means any individual engaged in the performance of work-

> (A) requiring advance knowledge in a field of science or learning customarily acquired by a prolonged course of specialized intellectual instruction and study in an institution of higher learning (as distinguished from knowledge acquired by a general academic education, from and apprenticeship, or from training in the performance of routine mental, manual, mechanical, or physical activities);

> (B) requiring consistent exercise of discretion and judgement in its performance;

> (C) which is predominantly intellectual and varied in character (as distinguished from routine mental, manual, mechanical, or physical work);

> (D) which is of such character that the output produced or the result accomplished by such work cannot be standardized in relation to a given period of time.[4]

This definition already embodies the long-established professions of law and medicine, but now includes the later professions of accountancy, engineering, clergy, dentistry, to say nothing of emerging occupations that fall or will fall within the penumbra of the definition, *i.e.*, computer programmers or "consultants". In the pursuit of the status of "profession" these and other occupations (particularly, teachers or educators) adopt as many of these characteristics as possible. Thus governing bodies are established, which promulgate a code of ethics and standards of admission to the membership of the bodies.

The crucial point about professional information or performance is the expectation engendered that it is reliable and successful—that it reaches a standard of skill. The closer the services approach compliance with the criteria describing professionals, the greater the expectation that a high level of skill has been exercised.

The legal issue in all of this is the extent to which these expectations engendered by professional status are translated into legal principles.

What the law of professional malpractice does is to make the professions more accountable. The rise of liability for professional malpractice is essentially

---

4   H.R. 6423, 97th Congress. 2d. Sess. (1982).

a recognition that professionals in all fields of specialty should be accountable to those who suffer harm as a result of their activities.

CHAPTER 2

Medical Malpractice:
Physician's Duties to Patients

The duties of a physician to her patient arise out
of the duties described in our previous Chapter _1_.
Because malpractice is essentially a tort action arising from an implied contractual relationship (although there are certainly examples of express
contracts between physicians and patients, but
these are so infrequent that we pass on a discussion
of this category of cases), we speak of the basic duty
of a physician to use reasonable care and diligence
in the treatment of a patient, a traditional common
law tort duty which may be reinforced by statutory
or contractual obligations as well. It is the set of duties a physician must fulfill in terms of diagnosis
and treatment which will be discussed in this chapter.

The first such basic duty is that the physician
should provide care that meets the standard of a
reasonable practitioner. This is another way of saying that she should have the fundamental qualifications of medical knowledge and skill to the same
degree as the average physician in her or a similar
area, which may be the local community or region
or state, depending on the presence of a statutory
standard specifying which. One court opinion put it
this way:

> "A physician should possess and use the
> learning and skill of an average doctor in his
> locality; should keep abreast of develop-

ments in medicine and should not depart from approved methods in general use.

The law relating to malpractice is simple and well settled, although not always easy of application. A physician and surgeon, by taking charge of a case, impliedly represents that they possess, and the law places upon them the duty of possessing, that reasonable degree of learning and skill that is ordinarily possessed by physicians and surgeons in the locality where they practice, and which is ordinarily regarded by those conversant with the employment as necessary to qualify them to engage in the business of practicing medicine and surgery. Another court stated that:

> ... The rule in relation to learning and skill does not require the surgeon to possess that extraordinary learning and skill which belong only to a few (practitioners) of rare endowments, but such as is possessed by the average member of the medical profession in good standing. Still, he is bound to keep abreast of the times and a departure from approved methods in general use, if it injures the patient, will render him liable however good his intentions may have been.

The physician is expected to be aware of the approved methods of treatment in general use and as the need arises must use them and thereby make them part of her skill. As new procedures are accepted she must adopt them. A physician who does not stay abreast of new and accepted changes or developments and applies earlier methods may be found guilty of malpractice for using outdated procedures that are no longer practiced in the profession. On the other hand, if more than one method of diagnosis or treatment of a condition is recognized, the physician can use either one, even though the one she chooses is not the newer or the most widely used, as long as it is approved by a reasonable minority of physicians.

If there is no established procedure, a physician may draw upon her own skill and experience and she is not negligent if the treatment is not successful.

A specialist is expected to have the higher learning and skill required to deal with a disease or condition. She is a physician who devotes special attention to a particular organ or bodily region, and to the diagnosis and treatment of its injuries and ailments. One is also a specialist who devotes special attention to a particular class of patients, like children or the aged. Most patients today seek out specialists for consultation and treatment and the internist has become the nearest thing to the GP or general physician who once dominated the profession. For this reason, it is appropriate to give further attention here to the duties of the specialist.

No state has established by law or statute any program recognizing a competent specialist. Each state requires a license to practice medicine, but the standards to be met by an applicant are such that she receives general authority to practice in any area of medicine. Thus a newly licensed physician can perform any operation whatever if she can acquire the patient's consent and secure hospital facilities. But as a practical matter, a physician is unlikely to get either if she dares to go outside her competencies. It would be an open invitation to a malpractice action without benefit of insurance protection!

However, the medical profession itself, through the American Medical Association, has established standards for recognizing specialists through the American Boards of Specialities. The following are specialties in which there is a national certifying examination:

> American Board of Anesthesiology
>
> American Board of Colon and Rectal Surgery
>
> American Board of Dermatology
>
> American Board of Family Practice
>
> American Board of Internal Medicine
>
> American Board of Neurological Surgery
>
> American Board of Obstetrics and Gynecology
>
> American Board of Opthamology
>
> American Board of Orthopedic Surgery
>
> American Board of Otolaryngology
>
> American Board of Pathology

American Board of Pediatrics

American Board of Physical Medicine and Rehabilitation

American Board of Plastic Surgery

American Board of Preventive Medicine

American Board of Psychiatry and Neurology

American Board of Radiology

American Board of Surgery

American Board of Thoracic Surgery

American Board of Urology

American Board of Allergy and mmunology

American Board of Nuclear Medicine

American Board of Emergency Medicine

Certification by any of the specialty boards has no effect in law. When the question arises in court as to whether a physician is a specialist the answer depends upon the facts offered in evidence on the issue. A physician who is a "diplomate" of one of the specialty boards is convincing proof that she is a specialist. A specialist may have no special credentials of certification and whose only special qualification is her own assertion that she is such. In law, a physician sued in a malpractice action is a specialist if she has held herself out as one, whether she is one in fact or not.

A specialist is required to have and use that degree of learning and skill ordinarily used by others
in a similar class in the same or similar locality,
having regard to the existing state of knowledge in
medicine and surgery. It is a higher degree than
that required of an average practitioner. This
means that a specialist should have a higher learning and skill, as one element, and should employ
the higher care, as another, of an average specialist
in her field. And of course she is expected to her
best judgment. Apart from the higher qualifications
and performance expected of a specialist, she is in
the same position as a general practitioner as to the
need for the physician-patient relationship and as
to the type of contract she makes with a patient.

Just as it does in connection with general physicians, the question is often raised as to whether the
standard of care required of a physician who holds
herself out as a specialist should be determined by
the practice within her profession generally or by
the practice among a geographically circumscribed
subset of her colleagues.

In a number of cases, the courts hold that a specialist is held to the standards of similar specialists
practicing in the same community. The reasoning
here is that a physician or surgeon who practices in
a small or rural community does not have the same
opportunities and resources for keeping abreast of
the advances in medical science as do the physicians and surgeons practicing in the larger, more so-
phisticated cities. However, other courts have held

that the standard of practice is to be determined by the practice in the same or similar communities because if the standard was limited to the community itself, then practitioners who were the only ones in a small community, and small groups of local physicians whose common lax practices fell far below that ordinarily practiced in rural areas generally, could be completely immunized from liability. It is further argued that in an age of ubiquitous national communication networks, increasing standardization of medical and specialist training and equipment, free flow of scientific information among medical institutions throughout the country, and professional journals and numerous other networks of continuing education which are national in scope, a national or nongeographic standard of care applied for all medical specialists. An apparent compromise between the views that specialists are held to local or national standards are the rulings in a number of cases in which the courts have expanded the scope of the geographic community to include the entire state.

A survey of some of the state laws dealing with the subject of standard of care in malpractice actions may be appropriate here. Nebraska defines malpractice as the failure to use the ordinary skill and care of professionals in a similar practice, in similar localities, under similar circumstances. Nevada defines malpractice as the failure to exercise the degree of skill and care that a physician uses in the community. Gross negligence and willful disregard of established procedures are defined as gross malpractice by the Nevada statute.

It should be noted, in connection with specialists, that physicians in general have a duty to advise their patients to consult a specialist or one qualified in a method of treatment which the physician is not qualified to give so that the patient might receive other or better treatment. The physician's duty to advise the patient to seek consultation arises when the physician knows or should know that she does not possess the requisite skill, knowledge, or facilities to treat the patient's ailment properly, or that the method by which she is treating the patient is not providing relief or effecting a cure.

A decision considering the duty of a general practitioner to refer a patient to an orthopedic specialist, stated that "if under the circumstances a reasonably careful skillful general practitioner. . . would have suggested the calling into consultation . . . of a specialist, the defendant was negligent for failing to do so." The standard by which the conduct of the specialist will be judged in referring or failing to refer a patient is set out in *Tucker v. Stetson*, 123 N.E. 239, where the court stated that:

> liability . . . in failing to advise (patient) seasonably to procure surgical relief elsewhere was not to be determined by jury on consideration of contingent, speculative and possible results of operation, but on proof by fair preponderance of evidence that it was reasonably probable such beneficial result would follow operation performed by defendant with ordinary skill of surgeons

practicing in towns such as that where defendant undertook to practice.

In calling for a physician's duty of care, the law does not require that she live up to the highest degree of care. As with learning and skill discussed earlier, the standard to be complied with is that of an average physician. This essentially means *reasonable* care and nothing less than that. What is reasonable care depends upon the circumstances of the particular case. It is the physician's departure from a good or approved medical practice that is usually enough to prove malpractice.

What we are talking about here is reasonable performance. A physician should be reasonable in determining the number of visits or treatments a patient should have and diligent in attending to them. She cannot abandon a patient, but must give her proper notice of her intention to withdraw.

The frequency with which the physician is required to see the patient depends upon the needs of the patient. In one case, the plaintiff consulted the defendant because of a swelling of the plaintiff's knee. The defendant treated the patient medically for about three months at which time another physician was consulted. Among other theories of malpractice, the defendant was charged with abandonment. The Michigan Supreme Court in *Fortner v. Koch*, 251 N.W. 762, held that the following would be a proper charge to the jury:

A physician is not chargeable with neglect in allowing intervals to elapse between visits, where the patient needs no attention during intervals, but he is negligent in doing so where the attention is needed. The frequency of the visits is a question for the physician to determine, if he uses ordinary judgment.

In the matter of the duty of exercising her best judgment, the law does not hold the physician liable for a mere error of judgment, provided she does what she thinks is best after careful examination. In medicine judgment is the faculty of deciding wisely, of determining what to assume and what to do at any stage of the treatment of a patient, using the word treatment in its broadest sense, in the face of unknown factors or others whose effect cannot be measured accurately. It is based on what physicians describe as "indications" and "contra-indications". A physician is required to use her best judgment in everything she does. She is required to do so in deciding whether she should handle a case or recommend a specialist. She is not required to use the best possible judgment that anyone could employ, but her own best judgment. But her best judgment cannot be less than that to be expected of one having the learning and skill of the average physician in her locality or beyond, depending upon the jurisdiction involved. Since as a practical matter if is difficult if not impossible for a patient to know or prove that a physician did not use her best judgment in a particular case, such a charge is rarely made.

PHYSICIAN'S DUTIES TO PATIENTS

Physicians have a duty of good faith to disclose to the patient the nature and extent of the latter's disease or condition, the probable course if the patient does not receive treatment, and the hazards and risks of the proposed treatment.

The issue of whether the physician obtained proper consent is essentially an issue of whether, under the given set of facts, the physician complied with the standard of care of a reasonable or average physician. If a physician intentionally misrepresents the seriousness of a procedure to induce consent, the consent becomes invalid, and the physician may be guilty of an assault and battery. If a physician negligently misrepresents the hazards of a course of treatment, he/-she then commits a negligent tort, and general negligence principles apply.

In one case the patient consented to a transurethral prostatic resection. In performing the operation the surgeon severed the patient's spermatic cords. The patient sued for assault on the ground that cutting the cords was a second operation to which he had not consented because he had not been told he would be made sterile. The court held that in the absence of an emergency the patient should have been informed before the operation that if his spermatic cords were not severed there was a possibility of infection, whereas if they were cut he would become sterile, then leaving it to him to decide what to do.

In another case, a patient sued a psychiatrist and his associates for fractures he sustained by undergoing insulin shock therapy for an emotional illness. The court held that because of the high incidence of permanent injuries sustained by patients receiving such therapy, the practitioners should have informed the patient generally of the possible serious hazards involved and there could be negligence in failing to do so.

Disclosure should be sufficient to assure an informed consent, but at the same time it should be limited to the extent deemed advisable by a reasonable medical practitioner, considering the patient's best therapeutic interest.

This duty of a physician to disclose is described in *Salgo v. Leland Stanford Jr University Board of Trustees,* 317 P2d 170:

A physician violates his duty to his patient and subjects himself to liability if he withholds any facts which are necessary to form the basis of an intelligent consent by the patient to the proposed treatment, likewise the physician may not minimize the known dangers of a procedure or operation in order to induce his patient's consent. At the same time, the physician must place the welfare of his patient above all else and this very fact places him in a position in which he sometimes must choose between two alternative courses of action. One is to explain to the patient every risk attendant upon any surgical procedure or operation, no matter how remote;

this may well result in alarming a patient who is already unduly apprehensive and who may as a result refuse to undertake surgery in which there is in fact minimal risk; it may also result in actually increasing the risks by reason of the psychological results of the apprehension itself. The other is to recognize that each patient represents a separate problem, that the patient's mental and emotional condition is important and in certain cases may be crucial, and that in discussing the element of risk of certain amount of discretion must be employed consistent with the full disclosure of facts necessary to an informed consent.

An example of too much disclosure is a case where a patient developed cancerophobia when a dermatologist told her that because of damage she had sustained to a shoulder from X-ray burns, she ought to have it examined every six months as the area involved might become cancerous. She sued the radiologists who had treated her. Besides recovering $15,000 for the shoulder damage on the ground of negligence, the jury awarded her $25,000 for mental anguish flowing from the cancerophobia. The dermatologist was not sued!

A physician has the duty to withhold privileged medical information about her patient. This applies to information disclosed by the patient herself and to what the physician learned about the patient from treating her. The purpose of this privilege is to enable a patient to freely permit her physician to learn whatever the latter wants to know. One legal authority describes this privileged information this way:

> The privilege attaches whether the physician was called by the patient himself, by a member of his family, by another physician or by an utter stranger, provided he attends for the purpose of giving professional aid and advice for the benefit of the patient. The fact that the patient was unconscious and unaware of the physician's presence is immaterial. The privileged relationship exists even though the employment of the physician was against the will of the patient.

The privilege belongs to the patient and she can waive it. She can accomplish this by giving the physician a written consent or authority to disclose the information. If the patient fails to object to the testimony of her physician on the subject when the latter is called as a witness in court, the privilege is waived. It is also waived when the patient testifies to the injuries or ailment in court, or when she brings an action and discloses her condition in legal papers.

This is a statutory privilege which is not recognized in a number of states while a few states have limited statutes dealing with the privilege.

CHAPTER 3

Medical Malpractice:
The Physician-Patient Relationship

It is fundamental that the relationship of physician and patient be in existence at the time the alleged injury occurred before a physician can be held liable for an act of medical malpractice. The creation of the physician-patient relationship takes place when the patient knowingly seeks and accepts the professional services of a physician for purposes of medical or surgical treatment, and the physician knowingly accepts him as a patient. As one court put it, "(t)he Hippocratic Oath, by which every doctor is bound, assumes a pre-existing relationship with patient and physician, which relationship in its inception is basically contractual and wholly voluntary, created by agreement, express or implied, and by its terms may be general or limited." *Osborne v. Frazor,* 425 S.W. 2d 768 (1968).

From that relationship comes the duties which a physician owes to a patient, the breach of which raises a malpractice action. The first of those duties is that the physician must use reasonable care that is expected of the average practitioner of his locality or beyond. The states vary among themselves whether the standard of care is according to the conduct of a reasonable provider within the state or whether the degree of care and skill practiced by a reasonable provider, in similar circumstances, whether or not in the state. Oklahoma disregards its borders altogether and set its standard of case by nationwide standards of health care. New Hampshire specifically requires its hearing panels not to consider locality when determining the standard of care in a malpractice action. Some state statutes hold the breach of the standard of care as malpractice. Nebraska defines malpractice as the failure to use the ordinary skill and care of professionals in similar practice, in similar localities, under similar circumstances.

If in a particular case the physician can prove that the relationship never existed, or that it had terminated before the patient acquired the condition for which he sues, the action would be dismissed even though the patient may have suffered serious injuries. Without that relationship the physician owed no duty to the patient and therefore could not have breached any such relationship. As we shall discuss in a later chapter dealing with defenses, proof that the relationship did not exist at the time of the alleged malpractice would constitute a defense.

Most patients become such by consulting a physician and being accepted for treatment. The arrangement is made by direct agreement between them. However, physicians may very well have other patients with whom they make no agreement yet the relationship exists. Children's treatments are usually arranged for by parents or guardians. This is true also of patients treated by corporation physicians and service people treated by military physicians. A physician who is serving in a hospital or clinic, or in a public facility such as a prison, normally has no agreement with any patient although the physician-patient relationship exists between them. This relationship is known as *consensual*. This means that it is consented to by both sides. This is true even when the physician is employed by a third person, since normally the patient must consent to the treatment.

Whether by direct agreement or otherwise, if the relationship exists, the physician is bound by all the duties that govern him as such. This is true whether he treats the patient without fee or the fee is paid by someone else or is never paid at all. The fee or its payment is irrelevant with respect to the duties of a physician toward his patient. Where the physician requires payment of a definite fee before accepting a case and the fee in not paid, the relationship never arises and he owes no duty to the patient. But once the physician begins treatment, even though he is not paid, he must go on with it unless he withdraws from the case by giving sufficient notice.

A physician in private practice is not compelled to accept a case. The license to practice medicine does not require him to practice at all, or on any terms other than those acceptable to him. In a case where a medical practitioner refused to treat a patient, allegedly in violation of a statute proscribing racial discrimination in the use of a public accommodation, the court said in *Rice v. Rinaldo,* 119 NE2d 657, 659:

MALPRACTICE

In the absence of a statute, a physician or surgeon is under no legal obligation to render professional services to everyone who applies to him or who seeks to engage him. Physicians are not public servants who are bound to serve all who seek them as are inn-keepers, common carriers and the like.

The rule that a physician is not required to accept a new patient does not apply when the physician is attached to a hospital, clinic, health plan or other institution where he must undertake the treatment of all patients who are entitled to medical services in such institutional settings. Under these circumstances, he is held to be in constant relationship to such patients. Failure to render needed medical services may subject the physician to a malpractice charge if the neglect injures them.

Thus where a former patient owes money to a physician, whether for medical treatment or any other reason, returns for treatment of a new condition, the physician can refuse to proceed with the case unless the old debt is paid first. But if he begins treatment without payment, he must proceed with it unless he withdraws after giving due notice.

The consent of the patient is also essential to the relationship of physician-patient. Generally, unless he proves that he acted in an emergency, a physician who treats or operates on a patient without his express or implied consent, is guilty of assault, a tort separate from malpractice. This is discussed in Chapter 3.

Most states have enacted legislation to protect health care practitioners who volunteer their services in an emergency from liability for damages suffered by the person whom they treated in the emergency. But whatever treatment is given must be carried out with due care. If the physician is negligent, he can be sued for malpractice in most states. In some states the statutes known as "good Samaritan laws" provide that when a provider renders gratuitous care at the scene of an emergency, he will not be liable except for gross negligence or wanton misconduct. California offers the greatest protection to such Good Samaritan physicians. They simply are not liable for civil damages when they act in good faith and without compensation while rendering emergency care at the scene of the emergency. Beyond this, California designates a special standard for negligence actions brought as a result of treatment provided in a hospital emergency room. Maine's Good Samaritan law covers some health care providers in some situations outside emergency circumstances. Any physician who provides services to a nonprofitorganization or a state agency in Maine, voluntarily and without compensation, cannot be held liable for any conduct less than gross negligence. In short, the Good Samaritan physician does not create a physician-patient relationship except for near-wilfull misconduct or gross negligence.

MALPRACTICE

Once the relationship is established, it lasts until the case is completed, unless it is sooner terminated by mutual agreement, or by action of the patient or by withdrawal of the physician. Duty of care requires that the physician-patient relationship lasts until the illness for which the physician is hired is concluded. A patient may discharge a physician at will either orally or in writing or by implication where the patient simply stops receiving necessary treatment, leaves a hospital against his physician's advice or engages another doctor. Where there is a discharge, the relationship is at an end.

Abandonment of a patient takes place when the physician stops servicing his patient while the patient still has need of those services. If the patient is injured as a result the physician can be held liable for malpractice. Generally, a physician is required to continue treating a patient until he has recovered, or has reached the end result, as after treatment for a disabling accident, or the patient dies. The physician does have the right to withdraw from a case, but he must withdraw properly so as to show that the relationship came to an end and there was no abandonment.

Finally, we must consider here the contractual nature of the physician and patient relationship. When a patient consults a physician and the physician agrees to treat him, they have entered into an implied contract. Typically, the patient comes to the physician describing an ailment and the physician treats it. Nothing has been said about the terms of their agreement, yet the law implies the terms. Nothing in writing is required. The contract establishes the physician-patient relationship.

The law implies that the physician will perform the duties imposed on him. As we shall come to learn in greater detail later, the principal duty is that in treating and examining a patient, he is to exercise the reasonable care of an average physician of his type, a GP (general practitioner) or specialist, in his locality or beyond, depending on the particular state statute. A higher degree of care is required from a specialist. The law further implies that the physician will treat the case to a conclusion, including post-operative care. It is also implied in law that the physician may have wide range in using his judgment and discretion as to what to do in the best interests of the patient.

Apart from the terms of the contract which are affirmatively implied there are terms that are excluded from it. There is no implication of any promise let alone guarantee by the physician or even the specialist that the treatment or operation will be successful or that it will not harm him or her or that the physician or specialist will produce a certain result. Nor is there any implied promise or guarantee that the physician or specialist will not commit medical errors, assuming that such errors, if any, are not the result of his incompetence or negligent (careless) performance. The law implies that the physician has agreed to render medical services, not to cure the patient.

MALPRACTICE

The law also implies that a medical contract can be terminated almost at will by either party. The patient can end his relationship with the physician and terminate his contract at any time. Almost as readily, the physician can withdraw from the case, provided he gives a few days' notice to the patient so that the latter can find another physician.

It should be pointed out that almost all malpractice cases are tort actions and the law of malpractice is a subdivision of a broader law known as the law of negligence. To put it another way, malpractice is known in law as a tort action founded on negligence arising out of a contract. Malpractice actions are rarely contract suits as distinguished from negligence suits because it is only in those few cases where a physician has expressly agreed to achieve a definite result or to follow a specified procedure that a contract rather than a tort action is brought. As a matter of fact such cases are, strictly speaking, not malpractice cases. In the contract case the physician may be sued for failure to perform the contract, no matter how careful he was. The typical malpractice case is one in which a physician treated or operated upon a patient without making any special agreement as to the result to be achieved. Something went wrong and the patient was injured or otherwise suffered damages. What we have, then, is a tort action founded on negligence arising out of an implied contract. For this reason the thrust of this volume dealing with the law of medical malpractice is the law of negligence and not so much the law of contract. Subsequent chapters will therefore address those aspects of the law of negligence which bear on the law of malpractice.

CHAPTER 4

Medical Malpractice:
The Elements of a Malpractice Action

It has already been noted in an earlier chapter that almost all malpractice cases are tort actions. A tort is a legal wrong committed upon the person or property of another, not ususally arising out of contract or involving a crime, for which the injured party can bring suit for money damages.

The law of negligence is in turn part of the law of torts. The elements of a cause of action for negligence in a medical setting are those common to negligence in general. Prosser's **Handbook on the Law of Torts** sets out those elements as: *duty,* an obligation owed to the plaintiff by the defendant; *breach of the duty,* failure of the defendant to meet the obligation owed to the plaintiff; *causation,* a close, causal link between the breach of the duty owed the plaintiff by the defendant and the injury suffered by the plaintiff; and *damages,* the sustaining of some compensable injury by the plaintiff as a result of the breach of the defendant's duty.

To Prosser's model, we include two additional elements, the first of which is fundamental in malpractice cases and the second of which appears occasionally but frequently enough to warrant inclusion in any discussion of malpractice law. The first element is *relationship*. The existence of the physician-patient relationship between him and the defendant as of the time when the injury occurred, from which flow the duties owed by the physician. This element was fully treated in Chapter 3, and will not be reported here again. The second element is freedom from *contributory negligence*. In several states this additional element must be proved by the plaintiff. In the majority of jurisdictions contributory negligence is a defense that must be proved by the defendant, instead of having to be proved by the plaintiff.

In an ordinary negligence case no relationship ordinarily exists between the plaintiff and defendant. The duty arises from the situation that confronts them at the time. In a malpractice case, however, the duty arises out of the physician-patient relationship. If it did not exist at the time of the injury, there is no malpractice case.

In a malpractice action, however, recovery against a physician is allowed only where there is a *relationship* of physician and patient as the result of a contract, express or implied, that the doctor will treat the patient with proper professional skill and the patient will pay for such treatment, and there has been a *breach* of professional *duty* to the patient. The duty of a physician to bring the skill and care to the improvement or correction of the condition of his patient does not arise from the contract, but has its basis in public policy that is inherent in the nature and exercise of the physician's profession. Medical malpractice cases generally recognize that the duty of the physician is founded in the relation that exists between physician and patient which is the result of a *consensual* transac-

tion, and not necessarily one of contract, the existence of which is a question of fact. Acceptance or undertaking of treatment of the patient by a physician
creates the relationship. However, the courts also
recognize limitations on the physician's obligation
or undertaking, such as that the physician is not required to undertake treatment of every patient who
applies to him. Since the question of the existence
of the relationship is one of fact, the courts have
been called upon in a great many cases to determine whether such a relationship existed under the
facts and circumstances of particular situations. In
situations where a patient has contacted the physician without referral, the courts frequently hold
that the physician-patient relationship was supportable under the particular circumstances. If the patient's contact with a physician came about from
the physician's position on the staff or as adjunct to
the treating institution, the existence of a physician-
patient relationship may be held supportable depending upon the particular circumstances. But
where the physician's contact with the case occurred as a result of his being consulted by another
physician, the courts usually hold that the physician-patient relationship does not exist.

Breach of duty, the second element of a malpractice action, means that there must be a showing
proved by the plaintiff that the physician did something contrary to the recognized standard of medical practice in his community or beyond according
to the jurisdiction's case or statutory law, or neglected to do something by that standard. Most mal-

practice cases revolve around some phase of the diagnosis and treatment of an ailment or condition.

Even where a physician does not have the basic qualifications of learning and skill such deficiency means nothing if he is correct in his diagnosis, treatment, or both. On the other hand, a physician with the highest qualifications may blunder in handling a particular case and so his diagnosis, treatment or both may be improper. It is proper performance that is crucial. The very essence of malpractice is failure of a physician to use the approved practice of the average physician of his type in a particular situation. Departure from that practice is the almost invariable way of proving malpractice, and it will probably be successful unless the defendant-physician can justify his conduct by special circumstances.

The third element is like the same one in any negligence law suit. It requires proof that the conduct of the defending physician *caused* the patient's injury. The causal relationship, or "proximate cause" is often more difficult to prove in malpractice cases than in ordinary negligence suits. Since the patient was ill when he sought medical treatment, it may be that the condition he complained of was just as chargeable to the original illness as to the defendant-physician's alleged negligent conduct in treating the patient. In a case involving the treatment of an eye into which a piece of steel had lodged, where the eye lens finally was removed, a court found the defendant negligent in not removing the particle. But the court also found that the defendant was not liable for the loss of the lens and the resulting loss of vision. The defendant produced medical witnesses who testified that even if the particle had been quickly found and removed, the lens would have had to be removed in any event. In essence, the court held that the defendant-physician's negligence was not the "proximate cause" of the loss of the lens and vision. However, the defendant was required to pay for the pain and suffering the patient endured before the particle was removed.

The fourth element requires proof of *damage*. Injury in a malpractice case is defined as any lack of a physician's skill and care which reduces the chances of the patient's recovery, prolongs his illness, increases his suffering. In short, makes the patient's condition worse than it would have been if proper care and skill had been used. The problem here for the plaintiff-patient is the problem of proof. Where the patient's injury is self-evident as where he has lost a leg, an arm or an eye, there is no problem. But in most cases it requires evaluation by expert medical witnesses to bring out all the phases of an injury not visible to a layman on the jury or to a judge sitting on the bench. The probable duration or permanence of a condition, the extent and nature of future pain and suffering, the existence of an internal or mental condition, the extent of the plaintiff's inability to do the physical work required by his job, the probability of other conditions developing from the present one, the percentage of loss of use of a limb or function, the aggravation of a pre-existing condition, the precipitation of a dormant condition, the likelihood that a condition will get worse in time-- these and other matters involving injury require proof which must persuade a juror or judge. Given the difficulty of getting physicians to serve as witnesses to testify on behalf of plaintiff-patients against physician-defendants, proving damages as well as causal relation between injury and the physician's performance is an exceedingly difficult problem for the plaintiff in a malpractice action.

The doctrine of *res ipsa loquitur* is often the last refuge of a plaintiff in proving the second, third and this fourth element in malpractice cases because they involve medical questions which almost always must be proved by medical witnesses, meaning physicians. Under this doctrine negligence may be inferred from the unusual character of the injury suffered when it occurs while a patient and his actions were under a physician's care and exclusive control. Three conditions must occur to make the doctrine applicable; (1) the injury must be of a character which would not occur but for an act of negligence; (2) it must be caused by an agency or instrumentality within the exclusive control of the physician; (3) it must not be due to any voluntary act on the part of the patient nor have been contributed to by him.

When these conditions for the application of the doctrine have been shown to exist, a *prima facie* case has been established. It then becomes the duty of a defendant charged with malpractice to prove (1) that the occurrence was due to a definite cause, unrelated to any negligence on his part, or (2) that the care given was such that the occurrence could not have been due to lack of care, but must have been brought about by unpreventable cause, although the exact cause is not known. Literally, *res ipsa loquitur* means"the thing speaks for itself". It is a method of proof or a rule of evidence whereby the negligence of the alleged wrongdoer may be inferred from the mere fact that the injury happened. Under this doctrine the happening of the injury permits an inference of negligence where the plaintiff produces substantial evidence that the injury was caused by an agency or instrumentality under exclusive control and management of the defendant, and that the occurrence was such that in the ordinary course of things would not happen if reasonable care had been used. To put it briefly, then, the words *res ipsa loquitur* refers to a type of case in which the plaintiff's proof permits an inference of negligence from the mere occurrence of an injury, where it is of a kind that does not ordinarily happen in the absence of negligence.

The fifth element in a malpractice action is the element of *contributory negligence.* This is defined as a breach of duty on the plaintiff to use the ordinary care that a reasonably prudent person would use and which is a legally contributing cause of the injury the plaintiff suffered. Contributory negligence is an affirmative defense that must be asserted in most states and proved by the defendant-physician. In a few states contributory negligence must be disproved by the plaintiff. The physician in such a case may argue that the patient neglected to disclose some relevant fact in his medical history so that it was impossible for the physician to properly treat the patient. In cases where there was evidence that the patient knew of the importance of the omitted information, yet deliberately concealed it, the courts have held that the patient was, or could be found guilty of contributory negligence. And in situations where the patient simply ignored an obviously important part of his medical history or chose for some reason not to disclose it, some courts have held that this constituted contributory negligence, thereby relieving the physician of all or part of his liability. The courts in these situations reason that a patient has a duty to exercise ordinary care for his own safety and should therefore volunteer any information which he knows or reasonably should know is pertinent and which the attending physician has failed to ascertain.

However, there are courts which have taken the position on this issue of contributory negligence that the burden is on trained personnel to ascertain all necessary information, and that the patient is entitled to rely on their skill. Such courts hold that the ordinary patient cannot be expected to know what parts of his medical history are important, and therefore need not volunteer any information and cannot be considered contributorily negligent for failing to do so. The courts have held that the patient was not contributorily negligent in failing to reveal information where the undisclosed facts were relatively unimportant and would not have affected the manner in which the patient was treated.

ELEMENTS OF A MALPRACTICE ACTION

A patient who deliberately imitated the symptoms of heroin withdrawal and begged to be given methadone, but failed to inform the treating physician that he was not an addict and that he had recently consumed a quantity of beer and a number of pills, was held to be contributorily negligent in causing his own death. The patient in this case, *Rochester v. Katalan*, 320 A2d 704, had been brought into the emergency room of a hospital where he stated to the medical personnel that he was a heroin addict and that he was experiencing withdrawal, and manifested symptoms apparently consistent with his claims. At the request of the patient, the defendant physician ordered that he be given a dose of methadone, and after repeated pleas of the patient that he was still sick and needed more methadone, the defendant administered a second dose. The next morning the patient died from multiple drug intoxication, after which it was discovered that he was not, in fact, a heroin addict, and that he had been drinking and taking other medications. Although indicating that the defendant physician had been negligent in failing to ascertain the truth before administering the methadone, the court stated that the patient had, beyond a doubt, contributed to his own death by inducing the physician to select the course of treatment desired by the patient. The court pointed out that even after the methadone had been administered the patient could still have revealed his true history so that proper measures could have been taken by the defendant and the other medical personnel to avoid ill effects. In conclusion, the court stated that it was the duty of the patient to use such care as a man of ordinary prudence would commonly use in circumstances like his own, and that he failed to do so willfully and intentionally deceiving the one treating him, and that he therefore could not hold the physician accountable for the consequences of his own lack of ordinary care.

The patient has the duty to exercise reasonable care in providing the physician with accurate and complete information and following his instructions for further care or diagnostic tests. If the patient fails to do so and such failure contributed to his death, the verdict will be against the plaintiff patient in favor of the defendant physician. A patient who failed to return to her physician when she had been told to return to have her breasts re-examined, that she was knowledgeable about the significance of breast lumps and who failed to reveal her history of breast lumps to physicians performing subsequent examinations was held to create a jury question on contributory negligence. It is therefore the duty of a patient to submit to the treatment prescribed by his physician, and to follow the necessary or reasonable directions given by the physician. If the patient fails to adopt the remedies or comply with the directions of the physician, frustrates or defeats the endeavors of the physician, or if he aggravates the condition by his misconduct, he cannot charge to the physician the consequences due distinctly to his own conduct.

Proof of *damage* is an essential element in a malpractice action. Injury in a malpractice case has been defined as any lack of a physician's skill and

care which reduces the chances of the patient's recovery, prolong his illness, increases his suffering,
or, in short, makes his condition worse than it
would have been if due skill and care had been used.

Damages is the amount which a jury or judge
fixes in making an award to a winning patient in a
malpractice case. The defendant is liable only for
the natural and probable consequences of his wrongful act. These are known as compensatory damages.
The physician defendant is not chargeable for anything on account of the original condition or ailment
of the patient for which he sought treatment, or for
the pain, suffering or anguish which arose from it.
If a procedure performed by the defendant is fol-
lowed by pain and suffering when it is carried out
with the requisite skill and care, he is not liable to
the plaintiff for that pain and suffering. Since the
plaintiff can bring only one action for his injury, he
is entitled to be compensated for probable future
losses as well as past ones.

Exemplary or punitive damages are damages on
an increased scale, awarded to a patient over and
above what will compensate him for his actual loss
resulting from the physician's negligence, where the
negligence committed can be characterized ranging
from gross negligence to wilful and wanton misconduct. As one court described such damages, "gross
negligence amounting to reckless indifference; wanton or gross negligence, such as bad motives or intent to injure the patient, or utter indifference as to
the effect upon the patient." *Los Alamos Medical
Center v. Coe*, 275 P.2d 175. In an Oregon case, *Gill*

v Selling, 267 P.812, the court, applying the standard of gross negligence, said that this negligence is characterized not by inadvertence, but "by an absence of any care on the part of a person having a duty to perform to avoid inflicting an injury to the personal or property rights of another, by recklessly or wantonly acting or failing to act to avoid such injury evincing such an utter disregard of consequences as to suggest some degree of intent to cause such injury." Accordingly, the court here held that the issue of punitive damages should have been kept from the jury where through a mistake of identity a spine puncture test was administered to the wrong patient.

The cases vary in their holdings as to whether exemplary or punitive damages for injuries resulting from unauthorized surgery or other treatment by a physician or surgeon is to be awarded. Where it has been so held to be applicable it has been reasoned it is sufficient that the act was an unauthorized trespass on the body of the plaintiff patient, which the defendant physician knew or should have known he had no right to do. A wilful and deliberate intention to commit an act which the physician was bound in the eye of the law to recognize as illegal can be said to constitute malice and to be violent, oppressive, wanton, and reckless even though there are not precise and technical legal meanings attached to such words.

But in other cases, unauthorized surgery or other treatment has been held not to warrant an award of punitive damages. In an action by a woman against

a physician for an allegedly unauthorized and un-
skillful operation, it was held that punitive damages could not be recovered where it was
understood by the patient and her relatives who
were summoned to the hospital and consulted, that
if upon examination by the physician it was found
that an operation was necessary, he would perform
it while she was under the anesthetic. Although the
patient had indicated before hand that she was adverse to an operation, the physician had a right to
understand that he was to perform it when there
was no evidence of bad faith, recklessness, or op-
pression on his part.

Most states stipulate that benefits a plaintiff in a
malpractice action receives from what are called
"collateral" or other sources are to be figured when
computing the judgment awarded as damages. New
York reduced a plaintiff's judgment by the amount
of payments the plaintiff receives from such collateral sources, less any expenses the plaintiff paid
during the previous years to acquire the sources.
Delaware also admits evidence of collateral sources
but not life insurance payments or other private
sources of compensation and benefits. Some states
allow evidence of payments from collateral sources
including insurance payments, government benefits, and employment programs. Judgment is reduced by the amount of the payments, less the
amount the plaintiff paid to acquire the benefits.

Payments to a plaintiff prior to judgment are usually not admissible in court, and they are not recov-

erable if the amount of judgment is less than the
amount of payments made.

States frequently limit the amount of a plaintiff's
recovery or a portion of the amount of a plaintiff's
recovery by statute. For example, Virginia limits recovery to $1 million in a malpractice action. A plain-
tiff in a medical malpractice claim can recover
$500,000 plus the cost of past and future treatment
in Texas. Only $250,000 may be awarded to a plain-
tiff patient for noneconomic losses in California.
Some states limit a health care provider's liability if
the provider qualifies for the protection of the
state's malpractice statute. It is evident here that
the reader is well-advised to check his own state's
statute in this matter. Furthermore, these statutory amounts are always subject to legislative
changes.

CHAPTER 5

Medical Malpractice:
Performance Grounds for an Action

Breach of one or more of the duties owed by a physician to her patient marks every malpractice action. Almost every malpractice case involves some element of the diagnosis and treatment of a disease or injury. The fact that a physician does not have the basic learning and skill is irrelevant if she conducts a correct diagnosis and/or treatment. Yet a physician with the greatest qualifications may nevertheless mishandle a particular case so that her diagnosis and/or treatment may be improper. It is the proper performance only that is important. An early court decision held that:

> . . . it is certain that, though he be the merest pretender to surgical skill, the veriest quack, yet, if by chance he treats the particular case correctly, he is guilty not of malpractice; and, equally, though he be a master in his profession, yet, if though neglect to apply his skill in the particular case he treats it improperly, the patient may have his action.

To prove malpractice the plaintiff patient must prove that the physician's performance failed to meet an acceptable standard of care. But the mere fact that a physician made an incorrect diagnosis will not render her liable provided the physician used the required skill and care in arriving at this diagnosis. This is true even though the physician ultimately treats the patient for the incorrect disease. A physician who negligently makes an incorrect diagnosis, but whose treatment is proper and careful for the actual condition, is not guilty of malpractice. But if a physician makes a diagnosis which is different from one made by another physician for the same patient, where there is no emergency, the former must exercise special care in order to avoid error before proceeding with treatment, since she is on notice that she may be wrong. If she goes ahead with treatment without reviewing the facts and her diagnosis turns out to be wrong, she may be held liable for malpractice should the patient suffer injury. Thus a surgeon might be guilty of malpractice in removing a breast that had no malignancy, despite the fact that before doing so she had conflicting reports from a pathologist, the first one finding malignancy of a test specimen and the second saying that the earlier report was mistaken.

It has been noted in Chapter 4, Elements of a Malpractice Action, that as in any case of negligence, in a medical malpractice case based on negligence the plaintiff must show that the act she charges was the proximate cause of the plaintiff's injury. Again, what this means is that the plaintiff must show that the act was so closely connected with the injury suffered as to justify imposing legal liability. In short, it must be a substantial factor in the injury. Simply showing that the physician was negligent will not sustain the action. An expert witness must testify and convince the trier of facts that the failure to diagnose resulted in the lack of or delay in treatment that caused the injury and that with treatment that met the customary standard of care, the plaintiff could reasonably have expected to recover.

Not incidentally, we should point out that the rule of requiring expert testimony is not applicable when the causation of the poor result is such that it is within the common knowledge of laypersons. But if the injury is one that is not traditionally within the common knowledge of a layperson, expert testimony is required to establish the cause. The Minnesota court in *Lorenz v. Lerche,* 196 N.W. 564 stated:

> . . . when the question is to be determined whether a physician or surgeon has negligently or unskillfully treated or operated on a patient, the standard to be given the jury is the usual and customary practice of the ordinarily skilled and careful practitioner in the community. Where the doctor has come up to that standard, the law holds him free from damage claims, even though it appears that errors of judgment is not what a certain practitioner may have done in a particular case. Hence special care should be taken that verdicts in malpractice cases are not made to rest upon a generally expressed opinion that a course of treatment was improper, unless there is evidence reasonably disclosing some specific acts or omissions which, under the standard mentioned, constitute negligence or unskillfulness, and further, that such negligence or unskillfulness, in the opinion of medical experts, caused the

suffering and bad results for which damages are sought and allowed.

Thus, like malpractice based on diagnosis, malpractice based on treatment must be proved to be the result of negligence where there was bad performance, not bad judgment.

A listing of the acts or omissions constituting grounds for malpractice which appears in the *American Law Reports Quick Index* covering *ALR3d* & *ALR4th* (The Lawyers Co-Operative Publishing Co., Rochester, N.Y. (1980) suggests the extent and variety of grounds for malpractice actions based on diagnosis and treatment:

- Anal or rectal disease: diagnosis or treatment

- Appendicitis: misdiagnosis

- Arthritis: negligent and deceptive practices in diagnosis and treatment

- Aspirin poisoning: liability for negligence in diagnosing or treating

- Battered child syndrome: civil liability of physician's failure to diagnose or report

- Blood transfusion: liability for injury or death

- Breakage of surgical instrument: surgeon's failure to discover

GROUNDS FOR MALPRACTICE

◻ Cancer: malpractice in connection with diagnosis

◻ Cardiovascular system: malpractice in diagnosis and treatment of disease or conditions of the heart or vascular system

◻ Confidential information: Physician's tort liability for unauthorized disclosure of confidential information about patient

◻ Diabetes: diagnosis, care, or treatment of diabetic

◻ Diagnosis or test: failure of physician to notify patient of unfavorable diagnosis or test

◻ Dressing: duty of physician to assist patient while dressing or undressing

◻ Drugs:

  -mistakenly administering drug

  -side effects

◻ Electroshock treatment

◻ Epilepsy; diagnosis and treatment

◻ Exercise or use of limbs: concerning instruction

◻ Eyes: eye surgery

MALPRACTICE

◻ Forced feeding: malpractice in connection with intravenous or other forced or involuntary feeding of patient

◻ Foreign objects

◻ Genital or urinary organs: questions of consent in connection with treatment of

◻ Glaucoma: failure to administer glaucoma test as malpractice

◻ Guaranteed results: physician's guarantee of medical results

◻ Heart attack: malpractice in diagnosis and treatment of diseases or conditions of the heart or vascular system

◻ Hemophilia: malpractice in connection with care and treatment of hemophiliac or diagnosis of hemophilia

◻ Homicide predicated on improper treatment of disease or injury

◻ Hypodermic injection: liability for injury resulting from negligence in making hypodermic injection

◻ Instruction: duty to warn or instruct nurse or attendant

◻ Limb of body: medical malpractice concerning instruction as to exercise or use of injured member

◻ Mental disease: negligent and deceptive practices in diagnosis and treatment

GROUNDS FOR MALPRACTICE

◻ Other organ: surgeon's liability for inadvertently injuring organ other than that intended to be operated on

◻ Preconception injuries to mother: liability for child's personal injuries or death resulting from tort committed against child's mother

◻ Pregnancy

-anesthesia, proof regarding

-cesarean section, physician's failure to perform timely

-informed consent: physician's duty to inform patient of nature and hazards of treatment in pregnancy and childbirth cases under doctrine of informed consent

◻ Prosthetic devices: liability in connection with insertion of prosthetic or other corrective devices in patient's body

◻ Radiation therapy -physician's use of excessive radiation

◻ Rectal disease: malpractice in connection with diagnosis or treatment of

◻ Surgical instrument: failure to discover breakage of

MALPRACTICE

▫ X-ray -duty to inform patient of nature
and hazards of radiation or X-ray treatments under doctrine of informed consent

-physician's failure to x-ray

Other grounds of malpractice which have been
considered among a physician's duties of care to her
patients will be reviewed here in order to make our
discussion of grounds of malpractice complete.

The physician is obligated to accord the patient
all necessary care as long as she requires it, and
must use reasonable care in determining the frequency of patient visits or treatments. The practice
prevalent in the physician's locality is the usual
measure. An unreasonable lack of diligence in attending to the patient which injures her is ground
for a malpractice action. Such a charge would have
to be proved by the testimony of an expert to the effect that the defendant physician's conduct was not
in accordance with good practice and that it was the
proximate cause of the patient's injury.

Discharging a patient as requiring no further
treatment when the physician knows or should
know that it is necessary, is liable if the patient is
injured as a result. The law holds that a part of the
proper treatment is the careful and correct determination by the physician of the time when the relation should terminate.

GROUNDS FOR MALPRACTICE

If a physician fails to use a recognized method of diagnosis or treatment of a condition she may be held liable for experimentation a not uncommon ground of malpractice in recent times. A physician is required to use established practices or methods. Failure to use such established practices or methods risks a malpractice charge unless the diagnosis or treatment turns out successfully. But if there is no established or accepted model of treating a condition, then a physician may exercise her own skill and experience, and in doing so she is not liable for negligence even though the treatment is not successful. However, before turning to a new form of treatment, the physician should obtain the patient's informed consent. In a Florida case, *Baldor v Rogers,* 81 So2d 658, a physician who treated a cancerous patient with drugs instead of the traditional X-rays or surgery was not held liable for improper treatment but instead for failure to inform the patient when the treatment proved to be ineffective. But while imposing an additional duty of disclosure, the court also praised the physician's efforts to develop a new treatment.

> We do have the conviction that the heroic effort being made by members of the medical profession and other scientists only emphasizes that an enemy so far is being fought in the dark and that one man should not be condemned from the fact alone that he chooses a weapon that another may consider a reed.

A physician, then, should obtain the written consent of the patient, after fully disclosing the facts to her, including the risk involved and that the proposed procedure is experimental.

It already has been noted that a physician may not "abandon" her patient or discharge her without reasonable notice at a time when there is still the necessity of continuing medical attention. In other words, where continued care is required of the physician, and the physician stops treating the patient, she may be liable for malpractice if injury results. There can be a termination of services before the patient has received all the treatment she requires but only proper notice. Termination without such notice is a breach of the duty of continued care.

Physicians have a duty to advise their patients to consult a specialist or one qualified in a method of treatment which they themselves are not qualified to give, so that patients might receive other or better treatment. This duty arises when the physician knows or should know that she does not possess the requisite skill knowledge, or facilities to treat the patient's ailment properly, or that the method of treatment being used to treat the patient is not providing relief or effecting a cure. In such case it is a breach of duty for the physician to continue to treat the patient. Since delay or not making such disclosure may prevent the patient from getting the treatment that would cure her and thereby prolongs or perpetuates ineffectual or injurious treatment. This would be a ground of malpractice.

CHAPTER 6

Medical Malpractice:
Malpractice Defenses

In our earlier Chapter 4 dealing with the elements of a malpractice action we discussed *contributory negligence.* A plaintiff in a negligence case cannot recover damages for an injury another inflicted upon him if he himself contributed to it by his own failure to use due care for his own safety. Such a plaintiff must pay the consequences of his failure to do so, even though the negligence of another combined with hiss to cause the injury. This is called contributory negligence. It is concurrent with the defendant's negligence. In a number of states, the plaintiff must disprove contributory negligence.

In a malpractice action the plaintiff-patient's contributory negligence may be failure to give an honest history, in not carrying out the orders of the physician, or in taking an affirmative action of a harmful nature, Failure to follow the instructions of the physician will not necessarily result in contributory negligence if a reasonable person could not be expected to follow the instructions because he was afraid of making his condition worse.

Ordinarily, a patient does not *assume the risk* of the negligence of the physician from whom he is receiving care. Under certain circumstances, even though the patient was injured by the physician, the latter assumed the risk involved and cannot recover against the physician. If a patient should insist that his physician undertake a certain treatment when the physician told him that the treatment was unnecessary and improper, but upon the patient's insistence undertook the treatment and the result was a permanent injury, the plaintiff patient could not recover because he had assumed the risk of the injury. Assumption of risk was applied in a case where the court refused recovery for the emotional distress suffered by a father who was present at the delivery of his stillborn child on the basis that "emotional distress was an ever-present possibility." Questions of whether the plaintiff assumed the risk is a question of fact to be determined by the jury. But if no reasonable jury could find that the plaintiff assumed the risk, then it may be treated as a question of law for the court. The defense of assumption of risk is not available where there was not full understanding of the risks involved, or that the acquiescence was not voluntary. Awareness alone is not sufficient to find that the patient assumed the risk. There must be a showing that the patient given his age, intelligence, and knowledge, he could be expected to fully understand the danger and its implications.

Res Judicata literally means that a matter has been adjudged, a thing judicially acted upon or decided. In a malpractice case an example of this doctrine as a defense would be where a physician sues for a fee and the plaintiff-patient counterclaims or defends on the ground of malpractice. The counterclaim would mean that the patient wanted to collect for malpractice. The defense would mean that the patient only wanted to defeat the suit for fees. If the physician wins a judgment for his fees it means that the patient's allegation of malpractice was rejected. Should the patient later bring a separate action for the same malpractice, the prior judgment would stop him because the claim had already been adjudicated and could not be made again. But if the patient did not raise the defense when he is sued for fees, it is an independent cause of action and future claims are not barred by *res adjudicata*. In addition, as part of a future action, the patient may sue and recover for the fees that were lost in the earlier suit.

A number of states require that a plaintiff in a malpractice case must serve a *preliminary notice* on the defendant within a specified period of time after the former was injured. This is usually a short time period and failure to serve such notice timely is a defense which requires dismissal of the suit.

A *statute of limitations* cuts off a right to sue after the passing of a specified period of time. This requires that an action be initiated before the time limit expires. In some states the statutes of limitations are tied into the date of the plaintiff's injury or the date of the act of malpractice for which there is a complaint. A very strict Michigan statute requires the malpractice suits be brought within two years after the physician stops treating the patient and his medical problem, regardless of when the patient discovered or had knowledge of his claim. Many states write extension periods into their malpractice statutes of limitations to accommodate special circumstances. New York requires that malpractice actions be brought within two and one-half years of the act complained of or the date of the last act of continuous treatment. The statute further provides that when a foreign object is left in the body, the plaintiff is allowed a time limit of one year to bring suit after he discovered or should have discovered the object.

Most states key their statutes of limitations period to the time when the plaintiff discovered or should have discovered the injury. The states that use a flexible period based on discovery and subject to an overall limit, also provide extensions beyond the limit for special circumstances. Almost all states toll the statute of limitations period when an action is being handled by a pretrial arbitration or screening panel.

CHAPTER 7

Medical Malpractice:
Screening Panels and Arbitration

During the 1970s, medical malpractice claims were being filed with increasing frequency, and the amounts of damage awards were reaching almost astronomical heights. As a result, there was a dramatic increase in malpractice insurance rates for physicians and other health care practitioners that made the premium rate structure just about prohibitive. Indeed, for those practicing in high-risk specialties such as anesthesiologists and orthopedists and surgeons generally, loss of coverage altogether was not unheard of. In effect, there was a "crisis" in the medical community which gave forth a flood-tide of publicity. There was tremendous sentiment that something should be done to deal with the inefficiencies associated with the traditional litigation process. Legislative action brought study commissions and statutes in just about every state. By 1980, the legislatures in almost all states had enacted some form of remedial legislation aimed at alleviating the crisis. Screening panels and arbitration emerged as an alternative means for resolving medical malpractice claims.

Screening panels are a pretrial device ostensibly designed to weed out frivolous medical malpractice claims and to encourage early settlement of non-frivolous ones. Before this "reform" movement, disputes were settled by the traditional tort procedures. Both plaintiffs and defendants have been dissatisfied with the jury trial, and physicians viewed it as the main factor in the increases in already high malpractice insurance premiums. Plaintiffs were disillusioned because the process was too slow and expensive, forcing them to settle quickly and for less than they believed they were entitled, and insurers were outraged at the excessive and unpredictable damage awards.

Pretrial screening panels which are essentially a form of non-binding arbitration, are a statutory creation in a substantial number of states: Arizona, Delaware, Hawaii, Indiana, Kansas, Louisiana, Massachusetts, Nebraska, New Hampshire, New Mexico, New York, Ohio, Pennsylvania, Tennessee, and Virginia. There are five general forms of pretrial screening panels: *Physician Screening Panels* which are controlled by physicians in closed sessions. Their objective is to determine whether a claim alleging malpractice should be defended or settled; (2) Physician-and-Advisory Screening Panels composed primarily of physicians but include representation by a lawyer, a clergyman, or someone from another profession in an advisory role. (3) Medical-Legal Screening Panels which are the most common and which may be regional or statewide. Physicians and lawyers make up these panels. (4) Court-sponsored Screening Panels administered by the court. (5) Statutory Panels established by the legislatures.

While designed to screen out nonmeritorious claims prior to the parties proceeding to trial, screening panels have no actual power to accomplish this result since their findings are not binding. Nor are screening panels used in lieu of the normal trial process but rather act as a condition precedent to bringing a legal action. If the parties fail to agree to the disposition of the claim, they are free to go to trial.

Screening panels operate rather informally. However, procedures in individual states range from adversarial trials with opening and closing statements, live testimony under oath, and cross examination of witnesses, to submissions in writing in which the parties explain their position and provide evidentiary exhibits. Pennsylvania, for example, requires that the panel abide by state judicial rules of evidence as well as state common and statutory law. Hawaii gives the power to pass judgment on the degree of the physician's liability, while Delaware allows the panel to determine how extensive the disability is, and Florida gives the panel power to award damages. On the other hand, Alaska and Massachusetts empower screening panels to rule on specific questions of fact.

It should be remembered that if either party is dissatisfied the screening panel has only acted to delay a jury trial, as already noted earlier. Some states allow panel findings to be admitted into evidence if the dispute goes to trial. This may pose a barrier to receivery when it is admitted into evidence or when panel members testify at the trial. In Kansas, for example, the findings of the panel are not admissible evidence but panel members may be subpoenaed as witnesses.

MALPRACTICE

After all is said and done, the use of a screening panel is a gamble. It provides the parties with a preliminary view of the merits of their claim and exerts pressure to settle. If not, everyone loses, for it delays access to the courts where the actual litigation will occur, and increases the overall expense. 1

The validity and construction of statutory provisions establishing some form of pretrial review panel to hear malpractice claims have had a checkered time in the courts. Where the constitutionality of such statutes have been considered it is the specific details of the statutory provisions that determine whether they are upheld. Thus, one such provision which established a screening panel composed of a judge, an attorney, and a physician and provided that the proceedings were to be adversary and like those at trial, was held to confer an unconstitutional delegation of judicial power on the attorney and the physician members of the panel. Some courts have held that statutory provisions for the submission of medical malpractice claims to some form of pretrial panel as a denial of the constitutional right of access to the courts. But a number of courts have rejected this claim. A number of decisions have held that such panels are a denial of the right to a jury trial and/or as a denial of equal protection of the laws. However, a number of state courts hold that a right to a subsequent trial re-

---

1   See "Medical Malpractice Screening Panels: A Judicial Evaluation of Their Practical Effect," Comment Note in 42 *University of Pittsburgh Law Review* 939 (1981)

moves any serious threat to the constitutionality of the panel.

Binding arbitration means that the award by an impartial panel is final as to the issues in dispute, enforceable at law, and subject to judicial review only on grounds of fraud, failure of due process, or defect in contractual provisions. Twelve states currently provide arbitration of medical malpractice disputes by statute: Alabama, California, Illinois, Maine, Michigan, Ohio, South Dakota, Vermont, and Virginia. Such arbitration of medical malpractice claims is voluntary. The parties freely and knowingly agree to submit present or future differences to a panel for final disposition. No state mandates binding arbitration at this time. Execution of an arbitration agreement may be drawn up before (proclaim) or after (postclaim) the claim is discovered.

Since a patient who agrees to an arbitration arrangement forgoes her right to have those claims grounded in medical malpractice judicially resolved, it is important that such patient have proper notice that that is what she is agreeing to. Most states have a notice requirement in the arbitration agreement, Furthermore, a number of states-Alaska, California, Illinois, Louisiana, Maine, Michigan, Ohio, South Dakota, and Virginia-require that the right of revocation of an arbitration agreement be specifically reserved within the agreement itself. The time limits for such revocation varies according to statute, 30 or 60 days being the usual time frame.

MALPRACTICE

As they do in connection with screening panels, constitutional questions or challenges arise under a system of mandatory arbitration. Again, the courts go in a variety of directions, always dealing with specific details of the statutory provisions in determining whether to hold them invalid. Predictability of outcomes is inevitably difficult. However, no state supreme court has found a malpractice screening provision to be in violation of the equal protection clause which is the most common constitutional challenge to panel usage.

CHAPTER 8

Attorney Malpractice

While it was not called "malpractice" at the outset, the liability of persons who professed competence in their callings comprised the first group of negligence cases in the common law. One of these "callings" was that of the attorney, and cases as early as the middle of the eighteenth century held an attorney liable on this basis. The attorney was liable only for "culpable negligence," and he was not responsible for mistakes. An early United States Supreme Court noted that "Attorneys do not profess to know all the law or to be incapable of error or mistake in applying it to the facts of every case, as even the most skillful of the profession would hardly be able to come up to that standard." *Savings Bank v. Ward,* 100 US 195, 199.

The desire to protect and compensate clients injured through the negligence of their attorneys as well as to provide an additional incentive to attorneys to exercise their professional responsibilities with care and prudence has led to the universal recognition of attorney malpractice liability.

Just as the physician's liability for negligence arises out of the physician-patient relationship, so does the attorney's liability for negligence arise out of the attorney-client relationship. Courts disagree on the underlying theory of the attorney malpractice action. Some hold that it is a contract action arising from the attorney's breach of an implied promise to use a reasonable degree of skill and care in the exercise of his professional duties. Others view it as a tort action that results from the attorney's breach of the duty to use due care created by the attorney-client relationship.

A Minnesota case, *Togstad v. Vesely*, 291 N.W. 2d 686, is frequently cited as a persuasive example of the definition of a client-attorney relationship which depends on the particular facts. In *Togstad*, the plaintiff claimed breach of fiduciary duty on the part of her attorney for negligently advising her that a medical malpractice action she wished to bring had no merit. She claimed that the negligent treatment of both the attending physician and hospital caused her husband's paralysis during a hospital stay. After less than an hour's consultation, the attorney advised her that she had no case. Recovery from both parties was later barred by the statute of limitations. The attorney defended on the ground that an attorney-client relationship was not created by his discussion with the plaintiff. The jury found that an attorney-client relationship had existed and returned a verdict for the plaintiff. The trial judge denied the defendant attorney's motion for judgment notwithstanding the verdict, ruling that there was sufficient evidence for the jury to reasonably to conclude that an attorney-client relationship had existed. The Minnesota Supreme Court upheld the verdict, finding an attorney-client relationship and consequent duty arising from it even in the absence of a formal retainer agreement or any other contractual factor when a party seeks legal advice from an attorney and relies upon such advice. The specific duty addressed by the court was the attorney's duty to investigate and fully inform the client. In this instance this would, at a minimum, have involved the attorney's obtaining and reviewing medical records prior to rendering his opinion, advising the plaintiff to seek a second opinion, and explaining his lack of medical malpractice expertise. In short, there is a duty on the part of the attorney to investigate and fully inform anyone seeking advice regarding the state of the law.

However, some jurisdictions will find that an attorney-client relationship exists only when there is an express contract:

> The legal relationship of attorney and client is purely contractual and results only from the mutual agreement ... of the parties... Such relationship is based only upon the clear and express agreement of the parties as to the nature of the work to be undertaken by the attorney and the compensation which the client agrees to pay.... - *Delta Equip. & Constr. Co. v. Royal Indem Co,* 186 So.2d 458.

Under either theory, the plaintiff-client must establish (1) that an attorney-client relationship existed; (2) that the defendant committed acts constituting negligence or breach of contract; (3) that the plaintiff was damaged; and (4) that the acts of the attorney were the factual and proximate cause of the damage.

MALPRACTICE

While the cases are replete with statements or suggestions that the relationship of attorney and client that gives rise to the duty to use care and skill and to evidence a requisite legal knowledge must show that there was a binding contract with a valid consideration. The first reported attorney-client malpractice case in the country in 1796, *Stephens v. White,* 2 Wash. 203, the court noted that "The most complete answer to the objection (that there was no allegation of consideration) is, that the appellee undertook to conduct the suit, and in his management of it, was guilty of such a neglect of his duty as to subject the plaintiff to a loss. After this it is not competent to him to allege a want of consideration." The fact of the matter is that whether a court uses a contractual analysis or the tort action theory of negligence, the elements of an attorney-client malpractice action remain pretty much the same.

No more than a physician, the attorney is not an insurer or guarantor of the correctness of his work or of the results which will be achieved. As one court's opinion put it, "Attorneys do not guarantee that their judgment is infallible, and are not necessarily negligent because they do not discover all decisions on a subject or may question their finality." *McCartney v. Wallace,* 214 Ill. App. 618, 624.

In pleading and proving a malpractice action against an attorney, the plaintiff-client must establish a breach of duty, that is, a breach of the standard of care. The standard of care requires attorneys not only to have knowledge of the law, but also to apply it with the skill exercised by careful and prudent attorneys in similar circumstances. The issue is not whether the defendant negligently disregarded, misapprehended, or misapplied the law, but whether the average attorney would have been as careless or imprudent as the defendant. As in the case of the medical profession, a lawyer is not liable in the exercise of discretion as to the better way to proceed or for a simple error of judgment.

One factor that is considered in applying the standard of skill and knowledge is whether the attorney is called on to act at once and without time for research and reflection, or whether he has an opportunity to look up the law and to plan his course of procedure.

The question of whether an attorney has breached the standard of conduct is treated as one of fact for the jury.

In suits for medical malpractice, it is the general rule that expert testimony of other physicians is required to give the jury a basis for making a determination. Although expert testimony is not demanded in attorney malpractice suits, experts do frequently testify about the components of ordinary skill and diligence. Expert witnesses in medical malpractice suits ordinarily testify regarding the degree of skill and knowledge of the average local physician or region or state depending upon the statute of a jurisdiction. The defendant physician will be held only to the standard of care customarily exercised by

physicians in the same community region or state
in the same field of practice. But in the attorney
malpractice cases there is no reference to attorneys
in the same community as the defendant and more
often than not it is the "ordinary" attorney possessing the same skill and knowledge regardless of
where in the state he practices that is the implicit if
not expressed standard.

There is no indication that the doctrine of *res ipsa
loquitur* is applicable in attorney malpractice negligence cases. Failure of success in a law suit is not
prima facie evidence of negligence or lack of proper
skill, Thus it has been held that "The mere fact that
a complaint turns out to be demurrable does not
show that the attorney who prepared it was incompetent or negligent. If he sets out the facts of the
plaintiff's case fully and in proper form, and the
question whether they constitute a cause of action
or not is fairly debatable, and after being so advised
his client desires to obtain the decision of the court
thereon, the attorney is justified in proceeding with
the suit." *Kissam v. Bremerman,* 61 N.Y.S.75. The
doctrine of negligence *per se* does not arise in suits
against attorneys.

The most common cause of lawyers' professional
liability claims is the attorney's failure to take some
action within a specified period of time. This is
known as the "time element error." Time element
errors most frequently involve the failure to file an
action within the statute of limitations. Attorneys
are held negligent for the damages claimed by clients in other than time element errors of course. Er-

rors in the preparation of documents such as drafting an unenforceable contract, failure to see that a will was properly attested (witnessed), and errors in the preparation of the accounts of an estate, are among such other errors that are held to be the cause of a plaintiff's damages. A listing of further causes of action against attorneys for damages resulting from their negligence includes: error in the pleadings; action in the wrong court; action on the wrong theory; improper service on the defendant or failure to persist in seeking to obtain service on him; failure to attach a lien on a debtor's interest in time; allowing a case to be by default; error in affidavit or publication of notice of sale; arranging for witnesses; conduct of trial in general; preparing trial findings and court orders, arranging for entry and judgment; actions to collect judgment; distribution of funds received; failure to follow client's instructions; erroneous advice as to legal liability and as to the settling of litigation; advice as to the condition of title to property; erroneous advice, in which client claims that desired results were not obtained due to poor counsel or advice by the attorney.

In order to recover in such attorney malpractice allegations the plaintiff-client must show that the attorney's negligence in these instances was the *cause* or the *proximate cause* of legal damage to him. Thus if the attorney overlooked an outstanding lien in approving a title abstract, his negligence is the cause of the plaintiff's being subjected to the lien. And if the attorney drew up a contract which turned out to be unenforceable, his negligence is held to be the cause of the plaintiff's loss in being unable to enforce the contract.

The question of causation raises its most difficult problems when the alleged negligence is in the conduct of litigation. The general rule is that when the client lost his case he must show not only that the attorney was negligent, but it must further be shown that the result would have been different except for the negligence. This has been called a "suit within a suit" because the client must prove that he would have won the first suit as one step in order to win the second one. If the original action was lost, the client must show that the original claim was a sound one and that he was entitled to recover on it. If the defense was negligently not presented in the original action, the client must prove that it was a valid one. If the original action was lost and the attorney negligently failed to make an appeal, the client must show that the appeal would have been sustained. Finally, it should be noted that the burden of proof on the issue of causation is on the client-plaintiff.

The measure of *damages* in attorney malpractice suits is compensation for the injury which the plaintiff suffered, and the burden of proof here is on the plaintiff to prove the damages. If the negligence resulted in loss of title to property, the measure of recovery is the value of the property. If it caused the overlooking of an outstanding lien, the measure is the cost of eliminating the lien. If the negligence is in conducting litigation, the measure of damages is the amount which would have been recovered had the defendant attorney not be negligent. Nominal damages, meaning where there were no actual damages, is rarely awarded in attorney malpractice suits. But punitive damages have been awarded, depending on the basis for such damages in particular jurisdictions.

The general rule has been that an attorney could not be liable to one other than his client in an action arising out of his professional duties, in the absence of fraud or collusion. This principle is related to the concept of "privity" which pertains to the relationship between a party to a suit and a person who was not a party, but whose interest in the action was such that he will be bound by the final judgment as if he were a party. In denying liability of an attorney to one not in privity of *contract* for the consequences of professional negligence, courts have reasoned that (1) to allow such liability would deprive the parties to the contract control of their own agreement, and (2) a duty to the general public would impose an unduly large potential burden of liability on the contracting parties. As far as this last reasoning is concerned, one might argue that if the court should go one step beyond the parties to the contract, there was no reason not to go fifty steps.

Although the weight of authority is pretty much overwhelmingly that an attorney owes no legal duty to his client's adversary the breach of which would support a negligence action, a few courts have reasoned although not always holding that an attorney should be liable under certain circumstances for negligence to his client's adversary for breach of his duty to conduct a reasonable investigation before instituting suit where it is reasonably foreseeable that a breach of such duty would injure the adversary. A number of cases have held that an attorney may be liable to an adversary for malpractice during the course of litigation which directly injures the opponent. By the same token, courts generally do not allow one attorney to place himself in the position of "third party" and, so positioned, to recover from another attorney damages for negligent conduct of a case.

It is fair to say that the present state of the law governing attorney liability to nonclients is far from settled. While the weight of authority, again, supports the strict privity rule, some legal commentators suggest that the trend is against this requirement. This strict requirement of privity of contract has been eased in a number of situations. The right of one not a contracting party to bring action for breach of contract has been recognized in the situation of a third-party beneficiary contract. However, there are cases in which attorneys are found liable to persons not their clients and cases where they are not so found, using the third-party beneficiary theory or analysis.

Courts began to recognize liability to third parties where a party negligently rendered services which he should have recognized as involving a foreseeable injury to a third party, at least in some circumstances.

In many cases, a "balancing of factors" analysis is used to decide whether or not an attorney may be liable to a third party non-client. The factors considered are: the extent to which the transaction was intended to affect the plaintiff, the foreseeability of harm to him, the degree of certainty that the plaintiff suffered injury, the closeness of the connection between the defendant's conduct and the injury suffered, the moral blame attached to the defendant's conduct (a factor sometimes omitted), and the policy of preventing future harm.

In many cases, nonclients have asserted liability on the basis of federal and state constitutional, statutory, and court-rule provisions. A number of cases have held an attorney's liability to a nonclient for negligent performance of professional duties based on federal or state securities laws. State statutes controlling the service of restraining notices on nonjudgment debtors in requiring one to pay expenses incurred by an opposing party by reason of failure to file or serve a paper within the required time, or a state constitutional provision conferring the right to make a will and have it carried out according to the testator's intent.

Generally, state codes of professional responsibility or similar state bar ethical rules do not form a basis of an attorney's liability to a nonclient. As one court stated it, using such a breach of a code of professional responsibility as the basis of a tort action would be "an oversimplification of the ethical complexities which govern the lawyer's conduct to his

client, the court and the public." *Spence v. Burglass,*
337 So.2d 596.

CHAPTER 9

The "Other" Professions
and
Malpractice

The concept of malpractice in professions other than medicine and law is one that has not taken a solid hold in the law. For the most part, law suits alleging malpractice in the practice of educators. clergy, psychiatrists and psychologists in particular are more often than not decided on theories of torts and contracts rather than "the law of malpractice." Then why bring up these other areas of the law in this volume on the law of professional malpractice? Our response to this is that in fact there are an increasing number of legal malpractice actions being brought against members of these "other" professions and there is and emerging body of law coming out from these cases which in time may very well be shaped into a body of malpractice law in those professions just as such a body of law has been built dealing with physicians and attorneys.

Educational Malpractice

It would appear to be a matter of common sense that a student who suffers harm when a teacher knowingly or negligently teaches him so that he leaves the classroom knowing no more than when he entered it or perhaps having been diminished through insult or ridicule that leaves him without self-confidence or motivation in subsequent years of his education, such student and his family should have a remedy based on malpractice principles to redress for these purely educational injuries caused by incompetent or careless teaching practices. This, however, is a highly controversial and unsettled issue in both educational and legal circles.

Until recent years, legal actions against school boards were almost exclusively concerned with students who suffered physical injuries as a result of negligently maintained school plants or poorly supervised gym programs or playgrounds. But as courts have become concerned with the availability and content of the school's academic program and services, they granted injunctive relief to students who were being denied services to which they were entitled. Thus emerged educational programs for retarded children, compensatory language programs for bilingual or bicultural students, and equal access to athletic programs for female students.

In more recent years, however, cases arose that urged application of conventional tort money damages to academic inadequacies in the public school. This meant a failure to educate a student in basic academic skills. Like most negligence causes of action, a failure to educate cause of action requires the plaintiff's proof of (1) a duty of care, (2) a failure to conform to that duty, (3) a failure to conform which is the legal cause of the injury, and (4) a compensable injury. It is a plaintiff's continual inability to meet these standards, among other reasons, which currently defeats the educational malpractice cause of action.

"OTHER" PROFESSIONS AND MALPRACTICE

The earliest reported educational malpractice case was *Peter W. v. San Francisco Unified School District* in 1972. *Peter W.* was the first suit in which a plaintiff had sought compensation for deprivation of what one legal writer described "one of the most fundamental necessities. . . the ability to read and write." In that case, the plaintiff received a high school diploma after attending the requisite twelve years of school. Despite graduating, the plaintiff was not capable of reading or writing past a fifth grade level. The plaintiff student contended that the defendant school district negligently failed to provide him adequate instruction, guidance, and supervision in basic academic skills, and failed to exercise that degree of professional skill required of an ordinary prudent educator under the same circumstances. Specifically, Peter W. alleged that the school district and its agents failed to recognize his reading deficiencies. He was assigned to classes in which he could not read the books and materials, and he was allowed to pass and advance from courses or grade levels with knowledge that he had not achieved the skills necessary for him to succeed or benefit from subsequent courses. He was permitted to graduate although he was unable to read above the eighth grade level as required by California law.

The initial justification for refusing to recognize the educational malpractice cause of action in this case was the inability of the court to find a set standard of care against which an educator's conduct could be measured. As the court stated: "Unlike the activity of the highway of the marketplace, classroom methodology affords no readily acceptable standard of care, or cause, or injury." The court reasoned that because so many variable factors influence the process of education, no single standard of care could be applied to educators. The court noted that the science of pedagogy promotes a multitude of conflicting views in determining the correct approach to educating students that as a matter of public policy to hold educators to an actionable duty of care would expose the schools to countless tort claims and ultimately result, in terms of public time and money, in consequences beyond calculation. There are numerous factors, both inside and outside the classroom, which subjectively affect a student's education. These factors include physiological, neurological, emotional, and more.

In *Donohue v. Copiague Union Free School District,* a New York case factually similar to *Peter W.,* a high school graduate sued his former school district for its alleged failure to provide the student with sufficient reading and comprehension skills. In denying the cause of action, again for public policy reasons, the court reasoned that due to numerous factors affecting one's education, proving causation would be a difficult, if not impossible burden on plaintiffs. "Recognition in the courts of this cause of action would constitute blatant interference with the responsibility for the administration of the public school system lodged by constitution and statute in school administrative agencies." The *Donohue* court concluded that the sole authority to make any educational policy determination was vested in the

New York Board of Regents and the Commissioner of Education, not the courts.

But the court here did not concede that an educational malpractice action fit within the strictures of a traditional negligence action. Despite this concession, Donohue's complaint was nevertheless dismissed because the court did not want to sit in review of the day-to-day implementation of broad educational policies. This reasoning loses some of its potency or persuasiveness when considered in light of the great amount of day-to-day policy-making activities that most courts are willing to review, such as those undertaken by doctors, lawyers, and accountants. This suggests that at the very least there does loom the possibility of educational malpractice actions becoming a legal action that may yet recognized by the courts.

But at this time it is clear that there is a judicial reluctance to recognize an educational malpractice cause of action . For one thing, courts find it nearly impossible to define any standard of care to which educators may conform. This is because there are too many factors outside the school environment contributing to a student's learning abilities and education. In addition, courts recognize there are many conflicting theories on how best to educate a student. For another thing, courts find it difficult to identify and measure the extent of any damages sustained by the student. Third, courts are unwilling to interfere with the operations of educational institutions (apart from equal treatment and opportunities in terms of constitutional rights), most of which already provide procedures for individuals to present their concerns and complaints about the education process. Another argument is that courts are reluctant to recognize the educational malpractice cause of actions for fear of placing increased burdens upon schools. Finally, courts hesitate to interfere with legislatively controlled teacher competency standards.

But while courts throughout the nation appear unanimous in denying a cause of action for failure to educate a student in basic academic skills, there may very well yet come a time when legislative recognition of educational malpractice will prove to be the most efficient means for redressing the injuries suffered from educational malpractice. The standard of care generally applicable to professional negligence action can be successfully used in the education profession as well.

Clergy Malpractice

The theoretical cause of action against a cleric for injuries resulting from his alleged negligence in the role and relationship of clergyman has been labeled "ministerial malpractice," "spiritual counseling malpractice," "clergyman malpractice," "pastoral counseling liability," "theological malpractice," and "clergy malpractice" as used here. This cause of action is intended to remedy an alleged error or lack of a standard of care in the counsel or advice given by a cleric as a pastor or spiritual advisor. Insurance companies have been offering malpractice insurance[1] to the clergy since 1979. One such policy of "Pastoral Counseling Liability Insurance" provides coverage to religious congregations and to "any pastor employed by the congregation but only while counseling within the scope of his duties for the congregation." The policy covers liability for damages "arising out of any acts, errors, or omissions because of counseling activities by a pastor. . ."

This policy excludes intentional acts. It also excludes coverage for liability arising from "any actual or alleged conduct of a sexual nature." Of course such conduct is actionable under a number of theories outside of "malpractice." A victim may recover under a theory of assault and battery, and if there is no consent, the spouse might recover for alienation of affections or criminal conversation.

In other words, at least at present, clergy malpractice actions focus on the professional counseling ministry of the clergy. This being the case, clergy malpractice cases so-called are rarely brought and when they are, they are decided on negligence theories and not on "malpractice" principles. A clergy malpractice claim is essentially a disagreement as to the proper conduct of a cleric's pastoral malpractice, which would hold ministers liable for the effects of alleged negligence in the giving of pastoral advice. The argument against this concept of clergy malpractice is that pastoral counseling is essentially a religious activity and not, as contended by some, just another form of psychotherapy. Therefore, standards of care applicable to psychotherapists are not applicable to pastoral counselors. Rather, the defendant cleric's denominational affiliation will control the definition of the standard by which his conduct is to be judged.

Of course the religious clauses in the Constitution are offered as conclusive defenses against clergy malpractice actions. Finally, there is the argument of public policy as a defense to the clergy malpractice theory. The clergy is exempt from licensing acts applicable to other counseling professionals. This would imply a policy that the state cannot and should not set standards of care in pastoral counseling which the courts would have to set up in order to determine whether there was a breach of such standard of care.

Actually what has happened is that the tort theory of clergy malpractice has expanded to become a convenient label for any cause of action against clergy. The term is frequently used in describing broader fields of offenses and action, including child abuse, theft, poor teaching and even paternity. Likewise, intentional tort and invasion of privacy are part of clergy malpractice today. Courts have always recognized that clergy are liable for negligence in secular activities such as negligence in an automobile collision, as well as for intentional torts such as false imprisonment.

On the other hand, parishioners cannot sue clergy for negligently performing traditional sacraments, services and other purely sacerdotal acts such as funerals, Christening, or weddings or Bar Mitzvah. However, courts have as already indicated, focused on ministerial counseling as an appropriate focus of clergy malpractice.

Since, however, the constitutional obstacles to holding a clergyman or clergyperson liable for conduct that results in harm to a client or parishioner can be raised no matter how the legal action is labeled, the term is elusive and inconclusive. No cases of clergy malpractice for negligent counseling have succeeded under a negligence theory. Very much like educational malpractice suits, the courts reject clergy malpractice suits. But given the number of suits which are nevertheless brought and the persisting legal literature on the topic, we cannot take it for granted that a time may yet come when these actions will become a part of the law.

Accountant Malpractice

Although certified public accountants are often involved in a number of aspects of their clients' businesses, including management consulting, executive recruiting, and performing a number of tax services, their primary source of revenue and activity is auditing. The accountant's special function is to scrutinize the financial statements prepared by a business and express an opinion as to the accuracy with which the statements present the company's actual financial position and operations in accordance with generally accepted accounting principles. The company itself uses this information in business planning and outsiders with an interest in the company need it to scrutinize the profitability of their investment.

APPENDIX A

Selected State Malpractice Statutes

APPENDIX A

SELECTED STATE MALPRACTICE STATUTES

CODE OF ALABAMA
Article 27.

Medical Liability Actions.
6-5-480. Short title.

This article may be cited and known as the "Alabama Medical Liability Act" (Acts 1975, No. 513, § 1.)

6-5-481. Definitions.

For the purposes of this article, the following terms shall have the meanings respectively ascribed to them by this section:

(1) Medical Practitioner. Anyone licensed to practice medicine or osteopathy in the state of Alabama, engaged in such practice, including medical professional corporations, associations and partnerships.

(2) Dental Practitioner. Anyone licensed to practice dentistry in the state of Alabama, engaged in such practice, including professional dental corporations, associations and partnerships.

(3) Medical Institution. Any licensed hospital, or any physician's or dentist's office or clinic containing facilities for the examination, diagnosis, treatment or care of human illnesses.

i

APPENDIX A

(4) Professional Corporation. Any medical or dental professional corporation or any medical or dental professional association.

(5) Physician. Any person licensed to practice medicine in Alabama.

(6) Dentist. Any person licensed to practice dentistry in Alabama.

(7) Hospital. Such institutions as are defined in section 22-21-21 as hospitals.

(8) Other Health Care Providers. Any professional corporation or any person employed by physicians, dentists or hospitals who are directly involved in the delivery of health care services.

(9) Medical Liability. A finding by a judge, jury or arbitration panel that a physician, dentist, medical institution or other health care provider did not meet the applicable standard of care, and that such failure was the proximate cause of the injury complained of, resulting in damage to the patient. (Acts 1975, No. 513, § 3.)

§ 6-5-482. Limitation on time for commencement of action.

(a) All actions against physicians, surgeons, dentists, medical institutions or other health care providers for liability, error, mistake or failure to cure, whether based on contract or tort, must be commenced within two years next after the act or omission or failure giving rise to the claim, and not afterwards; provided, that if the cause of action is not discovered and could not reasonably have been discovered within such period, then the action may be commenced within six months from the date of such discovery or the date of discovery of facts which would reasonably lead to such discovery, whichever is earlier; provided further, that in no event may the action be commenced more than four years after such act; except, that an error, mistake, act, omission or failure to cure giving rise to a claim which occurred before September 23, 1975, shall not in any event be barred until the expiration of one year from such date.

(b) Subsection (a) of this section shall be subject to all existing provisions of law relating to the computation of statutory periods of limitation for the commencement of actions, namely, sections 6-2-1, 6-2-2, 6-2-3, 6-2-5, 6-2-6, 6-2-8, 6-2-9, 6-2-10, 6-2-13, 6-2-15, 6-2-16, 6-2-17, 6-2-30 and 6-2-39; provided, that notwithstanding any provisions of such sections, no action shall be commenced more than four years after the act, omission or failure complained of; except, that in the case of a minor under four years of age, such minor shall have until his eighth birthday to commence such action. (Acts 1975, No. 513, § 4.)

§ 6-5-483. Elimination of ad damnum clause in complaints.

The ad damnum clause in complaints alleging medical liability shall be eliminated. Such complaints, in place of a claim for specific monetary damages, shall contain instead a general claim for relief. However, nothing in this section shall be construed to prohibit or restrict an attorney from requesting or suggesting a specific sum to be awarded during the trial of any medical liability case. (Acts 1975, No. 513, § 5.)

APPENDIX A

§ 6-5-484. Degree of care owed to patient.

(a) In performing professional services for a patient, a physician's, surgeon's or dentist's duty to the patient shall be to exercise such reasonable care, diligence and skill as physicians, surgeons, and dentists in the same general neighborhood, and in the same general line of practice, ordinarily have and exercise in a like case. In the case of a hospital rendering services to a patient, the hospital must use that degree of care, skill and diligence used by hospitals generally in the community.

(b) Neither a physician, a surgeon, a dentist nor a hospital shall be considered an insurer of the successful issue of treatment or service. (Acts 1975, No. 513, § 6.)

§ 6-5-485. Settlement of disputes by arbitration.

(a) After a physician, dentist, medical institution or other health care provider has rendered services, or failed to render services, to a patient out of which a claim has arisen, the parties thereto may agree to settle such dispute by arbitration. Such agreement must be in writing and signed by both parties. Any such agreement shall be valid, binding, irrevocable and enforceable, save upon such grounds as exist in law or in equity for the revocation of any contract.

(b)Pursuant to the provisions of this section, the claimant shall select one competent and disinterested arbitrator, and the party or parties against whom the claim is made shall select one competent and disinterested arbitrator. The two arbitrators so named shall select a third arbitrator, or, if unable to agree thereon within 30 days, then, upon request of any party, such third arbitrator shall be selected by a judge of a court of record in the county in which the arbitration is pending. The arbitrators shall then hear and determine the question or questions so in dispute in accordance with the procedural rules established by the

American Arbitration Association. The decision in writing of any two arbitrators shall be binding upon all parties. Each party shall pay fees of his own arbitrator, and split the expenses of the third. Arbitration shall be conducted in the county in which the claim arose. A judgment upon the award rendered by the arbitrators may be entered in any court having jurisdiction thereof. (Acts 1975, No. 513, § 8.)

§ 6-5-486. Optional method of payment of judgments in excess of $100,000.00.

Where a plaintiff recovers a judgment from a physician, dentist or medical institution, as defined in section 6-5-481, in an action for medical liability, and such judgment is in excess of $100,000.00, the court, in its discretion, may order that:

(1) There shall be deducted from the award, and paid to the plaintiff, an amount sufficient to cover his out-of-pocket expenses as well as his attorney's fee.

(2) The remainder of the award shall be paid to the plaintiff in monthly installments in an amount calculated to provide the plaintiff a lifetime income.

(3) If the plaintiff should die before payment of all of said award, the same income shall be paid to the beneficiary of the plaintiff for the remainder of the payments due.

(4) The defendant shall file a surety bond with the court in an amount equal to the award remaining after the expenses referred to in subdivision (1) of this section have been deducted. (Acts 1975, No. 513, § 10.)

§ 6-5-487. Advance payments by defendant or insurer not admission of liability; advance payments in excess of award not repayable.

(a) In all actions for medical liability, any advance payment made by the defendant or his insurer to or for the plaintiff, or any other person, may not be construed as an admission of liability for injuries or damages suffered by the plaintiff or anyone else. Evidence of such advance payment is not admissible until there is a final judgment in favor of the plaintiff, in which event the court shall reduce the judgment to the plaintiff to the extent of advance payment. The advance payment shall insure to the exclusive credit of the defendant or his insurer making the payment. In the event the advance payment exceeds the liability of the defendant or the insurer making it, the court shall order any adjustment necessary to equalize the amount which each defendant is obligated to pay, exclusive of cost.

(b) In no case shall an advance payment in excess of an award be repayable by the person receiving it. (Acts 1975, No. 513, § 11.)

§ 6-5-488. Rules of evidence and procedures in civil actions preserved.

All rules of evidence and procedures heretofore in effect in civil actions in the state of Alabama are hereby preserved, unless specifically changed in this article, in all civil actions covered by this article (Acts 1975, No. 513, § 13.)

ARKANSAS CODE ANNOTATED

16-114-201. Definitions.

As used in this subchapter, unless the context otherwise requires:

SELECTED STATE STATUTES

(1) "Action for medical injury" means any action against a medical care provider, whether based in tort, contract, or otherwise, to recover damages on account of medical injury;

(2) "Medical care provider" means a physician, certified registered nurse anesthetist, physician's assistant, nurse, optometrist, chiropractor, physical therapist, dentist, podiatrist, pharmacist, veterinarian, hospital, nursing home, community mental health center, psychologist, clinic, or not-for-profit home health care agency licensed by the state or otherwise lawfully providing professional medical care or services, or an officer, employee or agent thereof acting in the course and scope of employment in the providing of such medical care or medical services;

(3) "Medical injury" or "injury" means any adverse consequences arising out of or sustained in the course of the professional services being rendered by a medical care provider, whether resulting from negligence, error, or omission in the performance of such services; or from rendition of such services without informed consent or in breach of warranty or in violation of contract; or from failure to diagnose; or from premature abandonment of a patient or of a course of treatment; or from failure to properly maintain equipment or appliances necessary to the rendition of such services; or otherwise arising out of or sustained in the course of such services.

16-114-203. Statute of limitations.

(a) All actions for medical injury shall be commenced within two (2) years after the cause of action accrues.

(b) The date of the accrual of the cause of action shall be the date of the wrongful act complained of and no other time. However, where the action is based upon the discovery of a foreign object in the body of the injured person which is not discovered and could not reasonably have been discovered within such two-year period, the action may be commenced within one (1) year from the date of discovery or the date the foreign object reasonably should have been discovered, whichever is earlier.

(c) A minor under the age of eighteen (18) years at the time of the act, omission, or failure complained of, shall in any event have until his nineteenth birthday in which to commence an action.

(d) Any person who had been adjudicated incompetent at the time of the act, omission, or failure complained of, shall have until one (1) year after that disability is removed in which to commence an action.

16-114-204. Notice of intent to sue.

(a) No action for medical injury shall be commenced until at least sixty (60) days after service upon the person or persons alleged to be liable, by certified or registered mail to the last known address of the person or persons allegedly liable, of a written notice of the alleged injuries and the damages claimed.

(b) If the notice is served within sixty (60) days of the expiration of the period for bringing suit described in § 16-114-203, the time for commencement of the action shall be extended seventy (70) days from the service of the notice.

16-114-205. Allegation of damages.

(a) In any action for medical injury, the declaration or other affirmative pleading shall not specify the amount of damages claimed but shall, instead, contain a general allegation of damage and shall state that the damages claimed are within any minimum or maximum jurisdictional limits of the court to which the pleading is addressed.

(b) At any time after service of the pleading, the defendant may, by special interrogatory, demand a statement of the amount of damages claimed by the plaintiff, which shall be answered within thirty (30) days.

16-114-206. Burden of proof.

(a) In any action for medical injury, the plaintiff shall have the burden of proving:

(1) The degree of skill and learning ordinarily possessed and used by members of the profession of the medical care provider in good standing, engaged in the same type of practice or specialty in the locality in which he practices or in a similar locality;

(2) That the medical care provider failed to act in accordance with that standard; and

(3) That as a proximate result thereof, the injured person suffered injuries which would not otherwise have occurred.

(b)(1) Without limiting the applicability of subsection (a) of this section, where the plaintiff claims that a medical care provider failed to supply adequate information to obtain the informed consent of the injured person, the plaintiff shall have the burden of proving that the treatment, procedure, or surgery was performed in other than an emergency situation and that the medical care provider did not supply that type of information regarding the treatment, procedure, or surgery as would customarily have been given to a patient in the position of the injured person or other persons authorized to give consent for such a patient by other medical care providers with similar training and experience at the time of the treatment, procedure, or surgery in the locality in which the medical care provider practices or in a similar locality.

(2) In determining whether the plaintiff has satisfied the requirements of subdivision (b)(1) of this section, the following matters shall also be considered as material issues:

(A) Whether a person of ordinary intelligence and awareness in a position similar to that of the injured person or persons giving consent on his behalf could reasonably be expected to know of the risks or hazards inherent in such treatment, procedure, or surgery;

(B) Whether the injured party or the person giving consent on his behalf knew of the risks or hazards inherent in such treatment, procedure, or surgery;

(C) Whether it was reasonable for the medical care provider to limit disclosure of information because such disclosure could be expected to adversely and substantially affect the injured person's condition.

16-114-207. Expert witnesses.

In any action for medical injury:

(1) Rule 702 of the Uniform Rules of Evidence shall govern the qualifications of expert witnesses;

(2) No witness whose compensation for his services is in any way dependent on the outcome of the case shall be permitted to give expert testimony;

(3) No medical care provider shall be required to give expert opinion testimony against himself or herself as to any of the matters set forth in § 16-114-206 at a trial. However, this shall not apply to discovery. Discovery information can be used at a trial as in other lawsuits.

16-114-208. Damage awards - Periodic payment of future damages.

(a)(1) The damages awarded may include compensation for actual economic losses recognized by law suffered by the injured person by reason of medical injury including, but not limited to, the cost of reasonable and necessary medical services, rehabilitation services, custodial care, loss of services, and loss of earnings or earning capacity;

(2) The damages awarded may include compensation for pain and suffering and other noneconomic loss recognized by law;

(b) In the event of a verdict for the plaintiff, the finder of fact shall separately state its awards for both past and future economic losses and for both past and future noneconomic losses;

(c)(1) In the event of a judgment for the plaintiff, if the award for future damages exceeds one hundred thousand dollars ($100,000) the court may, at the request of either party, order that the future damages of the injured person exceeding one hundred thousand dollars ($100,000) be paid in whole, or in part, by periodic payments as determined by the court, rather than by lump sum payment, on such terms as the court deems just and equitable.

(2) As a condition to authorizing periodic payments of future damages, the court may order a judgment debtor who is not adequately insured to post security adequate to assure full payment of such damages.

(3) In the event of the death of the injured person prior to completion of installment payments of principal and interest upon motion of any party in interest, the court shall modify the order by deducting from the remaining balance the amount representing unpaid compensation for future pain and suffering and future expenses of care and by ordering the remainder to be paid into and become a part of the estate of the decedent.

16-114-209. False and unreasonable pleadings.

If in any action for medical injury, claims, defenses, or denials are intentionally made without reasonable cause and found to be untrue, the party pleading them shall thereafter be subject to the payment of reasonable costs actually incurred by the other party by reason of the untrue pleading.

CONNECTICUT GENERAL STATUTES ANNOTATED

§ 52-184b. Failure to bill and advance payments inadmissible in malpractice cases

(a) For the purposes of this section, "health care provider" means any person, corporation, facility or institution licensed by this state to provide health care or professional services, or an officer, employee or agent thereof acting in the course and scope of his employment.

(b) The failure of a health care provider to bill a patient for services rendered shall not be construed as an admission of liability and shall not be admissible in evidence as to liability in any trial for malpractice, error or omission against a health care provider in connection with the provision of health care or professional services.

(c) Any advance payment for medical bills by a health care provider or by the insurer of a health care provider shall not be construed as an admission of liability and shall not be admissible in evidence as to liability in any trial for malpractice, error or omission against a health care provider in connection with the provision of health care or professional services.

§ 52-184c. Standard of care in negligence action against health care provider. Qualifications of expert witness

(a) In any civil action to recover damages resulting from personal injury or wrongful death occurring on or after October 1, 1987, in which it is alleged that such injury or death resulted from the negligence of a health care provider, as defined in section 52-184b, the claimant shall have the burden of proving by the preponderance of the evidence that the alleged actions of the health care provider represented a breach of the prevailing professional standard of care for that health care provider. The prevailing professional standard of care for a given health care provider shall be that level of care, skill and treatment which, in light of all relevant surrounding circumstances, is recognized as acceptable and appropriate by reasonably prudent similar health care providers.

(b) If the defendant health care provider is not certified by the appropriate American board as being a specialist, is not trained and experienced in a medical specialty, or does not hold himself out as a specialist, a "similar health care provider" in one who: (1) Is licensed by the appropriate regulatory agency of this state or another state requiring the same or greater qualifications; and (2) is trained and experienced in the same discipline or school of practice and such training and experience shall be as a result of the active involvement in the practice or teaching of medicine within the five-year period before the incident giving rise to the claim.

(c) If the defendant health care provider is certified by the appropriate American board as a specialist, is trained and experienced in a medical specialty, or holds himself out as a specialist, a "similar health care provider" is one who: (1) Is trained and experienced in the same specialty; and (2) is certified by the appropriate American board in the same specialty; provided if the defendant health care provider is providing treatment or diagnosis for a condition which is not within his specialty, a specialist trained in the treatment or diagnosis for that condition shall be considered a "similar health care provider".

(d) Any health care provider may testify as an expert in any action if he: (1) Is a "similar health care provider" pursuant to subsection (b) or (c) of this section; or (2) is not a similar health care provider pursuant to subsection (b) or (c) of this section but, to the satisfaction of the court, possesses sufficient training, experience and knowledge as a result of practice or teaching in a related field of medicine, so as to be able to provide such expert testimony as to the prevailing professional standard of care in a given field of medicine. Such training, experience or knowledge shall be as a result of the active involvement in the practice or teaching of medicine within the five-year period before the incident giving rise to the claim.

DELAWARE CODE ANNOTATED

§ 6851. Agreement assuring result to be in writing.

No liability shall be imposed upon any health care provider on the basis of an alleged breach of contract, express or implied, assuring results to be obtained from undertaking or not undertaking any diagnostic or therapeutic procedure in the course of health care, unless such contract is set forth in writing and signed by such health care provider or by an authorized agent of such health care provider. (60 Del. Laws, c. 373, § 1.)

§ 6852. Informed consent.

(a) No recovery of damages based upon a lack of informed consent shall be allowed in any action for malpractice unless:

(1) The injury alleged involved a nonemergency treatment, procedure or surgery; and

(2) The injured party proved by a preponderance of evidence that the health care provider did not supply information regarding such treatment, procedure or surgery to the extent customarily given to patients, or other persons authorized to give consent for patients, by other licensed health care providers with similar training and/or experience in the same or similar health care communities as that of the defendant at the time of the treatment, procedure or surgery.

In any action for malpractice, in addition to other defenses provided by law, it shall be a defense to any allegation that such health care provider treated, examined or otherwise rendered professional care to an injured party without his or her informed consent that:

APPENDIX A

(1) A person of ordinary intelligence and awareness in a position similar to that of the injured party could reasonably be expected to appreciate and comprehend hazards inherent in such treatment;

(2) The injured party assured the health care provider he or she would undergo the treatment regardless of the risk involved or that he or she did not want to be given the information or any part thereof to which he or she could otherwise be entitled; or

(3) It was reasonable for the health care provider to limit the extent of his or her disclosures of the risks of the treatment, procedure or surgery to the injured party because further disclosure could be expected to affect, adversely and substantially, the injured party's condition, or the outcome of the treatment, procedure or surgery. (60 Del. Laws, c. 373, § 1.)

§ 6853. Requirement of expert medical testimony.

No liability shall be based upon asserted negligence unless expert medical testimony is presented as to the alleged deviation from the applicable standard of care in the specific circumstances of the case and as to the causation of the alleged personal injury or death, except that such expert medical testimony shall not be required if a malpractice review panel has found negligence to have occurred and to have caused the alleged personal injury or death and the opinion of such panel is admitted into evidence; provided, however, that a rebuttable inference that personal injury or death was caused by negligence shall arise where evidence is presented that the personal injury or death occurred in any 1 or more of the following circumstances: (1) A foreign object was unintentionally left within the body of the patient following surgery; (2) an explosion or fire originating in a substance used in treatment occurred in the course of treatment; or (3) a surgical procedure was performed on the wrong patient or the wrong organ, limb or part of the patient's body. Except as otherwise provided herein, there shall be no inference or presumption of negligence on the part of a health care provider. (60 Del. Laws, c. 373, § 1.)

§ 6854. Expert witness.

(a) No person shall be competent to give expert medical testimony as to applicable standards of skill and care unless such person is familiar with that degree of skill ordinarily employed in the community or locality where the alleged malpractice occurred, under similar circumstances, by members of the profession practiced by the health care provider; provided, however, that any such expert witness need not be licensed in the State.

(b) Any physician who has been in the active practice of medicine or surgery for at least the past 5 years and who currently practices in the State or within a state contiguous to the State and within a radius of 75 miles of the Capitol of the State shall be presumed to be competent to give expert medical testimony as to applicable standards of skill and care, if it shall be established that the degree of skill and care required of the expert in the locality where the expert practices or teaches is of the same or equivalent standard as the skill and care employed in the community or locality where the alleged malpractice occurred (60 Del. Laws, c. 373, § 1; 62 Del. Laws, c. 274, § 1.)

§ 6855. Punitive damages.

In any action for malpractice, punitive damages may be awarded only if it is found that the injury complained of was maliciously intended or was the result of wilful or wanton misconduct by the health care provider, and may be awarded only if separately awarded by the trier of fact in a separate finding from any finding of compensatory damages which separate finding shall also state the amounts being awarded for each such category of damages. Injuries shall not be considered maliciously intended in instances in which unforeseen damage or injury results from intended medication, manipulation, surgery, treatment or the intended omission thereof, administered or omitted without actual malice or if the intended treatment is applied or omitted by mistake to or for the wrong patient or wrong organ. (60 Del. Laws, c. 373, § 1.)

§ 6856. General limitations.

No action for the recovery of damages upon a claim against a health care provider for personal injury, including personal injury which results in death, arising out of malpractice shall be brought after the expiration of 2 years from the date upon which such injury occurred; provided, however, that:

(1) Solely in the event of personal injury the occurrence of which, during such period of 2 years, was unknown to and could not in the exercise of reasonable diligence have been discovered by the injured person, such action may be brought prior to the expiration of 3 years from the date upon which such injury occurred, and not thereafter; and

(2) A minor under the age of 6 years shall have until the latter of time for bringing such an action as provided for hereinabove or until the minor's 6th birthday in which to bring an action. (60 Del. Laws, c. 373, § 1.)

SELECTED STATE STATUTES

WEST'S FLORIDA STATUTES ANNOTATED

766.102. Medical negligence; standards of recovery

(1) In any action for recovery of damages based on the death or personal injury of any person in which it is alleged that such death or injury resulted from the negligence of a health care provider as defined in s. 768.50(2)(b), the claimant shall have the burden of proving by the greater weight of evidence that the alleged actions of the health care provider represented a breach of the prevailing professional standard of care for that health care provider. The prevailing professional standard of care for a given health care provider shall be that level of care, skill, and treatment which, in light of all relevant surrounding circumstances, is recognized as acceptable and appropriate by reasonably prudent similar health care providers.

(2)(a) If the health care provider whose negligence is claimed to have created the cause of action is not certified by the appropriate American board as being a specialist, is not trained and experienced in a medical specialty, or does not hold himself out as a specialist, a "similar health care provider" is one who:

1. Is licensed by the appropriate regulatory agency of this state;

2. Is trained and experienced in the same discipline or school of practice; and

3. Practices in the same or similar medical community.

(b). If the health care provider whose negligence is claimed to have created the cause of action is certified by the appropriate American board as a specialist, is trained and experienced in a medical specialty, or holds himself out as a specialist, a "similar health care provider" is one who:

1. Is trained and experienced in the same specialty; and

2. Is certified by the appropriate American board in the same specialty. However, if any health care provider described in this paragraph is providing treatment or diagnosis for a condition which is not within his specialty, a specialist trained in the treatment or diagnosis for that condition shall be considered a "similar health care provider."

(c)The purpose of this subsection is to establish a relative standard of care for various categories and classifications of health care providers. Any health care provider may testify as an expert in any action if he:

1. Is a similar health care provider pursuant to paragraph (a) or paragraph (b); or

2. Is not a similar health care provider pursuant to paragraph (a) or paragraph (b) but, to the satisfaction of the court, possesses sufficient training, experience, and knowledge as a result of practice or teaching in the specialty of the defendant or practice or teaching in a related field of medicine, so as to be able to provide such expert testimony as to the prevailing professional standard of care in a given field of medicine. Such training, experience, or knowledge must be as a result of the active involvement in the practice or teaching of medicine within the 5-year period before the incident giving rise to the claim.

(3)(a) If the injury is claimed to have resulted from the negligent affirmative medical intervention of the health care provider, the claimant must, in order to prove a breach of the prevailing professional standard of care, show that the injury was not within the necessary or reasonably foreseeable results of the surgical, medicinal, or diagnostic procedure constituting the medical intervention, if the intervention from which the injury is alleged to have resulted was carried out in accordance with the prevailing professional standard of care by a reasonably prudent similar health care provider. (b) The provisions of this subsection shall apply only when the medical intervention was undertaken with the informed consent of the patient in compliance with the provisions of s. 766.103.

(4) The existence of a medical injury shall not create any inference or presumption of negligence against a health care provider, and the claimant must maintain the burden of proving that an injury was proximately caused by a breach of the prevailing professional standard of care by the health care provider. However, the discovery of the presence of a foreign body, such as a sponge, clamp, forceps, surgical needle, or other paraphernalia commonly used in surgical, examination, or diagnostic procedures, shall be prima facie evidence of negligence on the part of the health care provider.

(5) The Legislature is cognizant of the changing trends and techniques for the delivery of health care in this state and the discretion that is inherent in the diagnosis, care, and treatment of patients by different health care providers. The failure of a health care provider to order, perform, or administer supplemental diagnostic tests shall not be actionable if the health care provider acted in good faith and with due regard for the prevailing professional standard of care.

(6)(a) In any action for damages involving a claim of negligence against a physician licensed under chapter 458, osteopathic physician licensed under chapter 459, podiatrist licensed under chapter 461, or chiropractor licensed under chapter 460 providing emergency medical services in a hospital emergency department, the court shall admit expert medical testimony only from physicians, osteopathic physicians, podiatrists, and chiropractors who have had substantial professional experience within the preceding 5 years while assigned to provide emergency medical services in a hospital emergency department.

APPENDIX A

(b)For the purposes of this subsection:

1. The term "emergency medical services" means those medical services required for the immediate diagnosis and treatment of medical conditions which, if not immediately diagnosed and treated, could lead to serious physical or mental disability or death.

2. "Substantial professional experience" shall be determined by the custom and practice of the manner in which emergency medical coverage is provided in hospital emergency departments in the same or similar localities where the alleged negligence occurred.

766.103. Florida Medical Consent Law

(1) This section shall be known and cited as the "Florida Medical Consent Law."

(2) In any medical treatment activity not covered by s. 768.13, entitled the "Good Samaritan Act," this act shall govern.

(3) No recovery shall be allowed in any court in this state against any physician licensed under chapter 458, osteopath licensed under chapter 459, chiropractor licensed under chapter 460, podiatrist licensed under chapter 461, or dentist licensed under chapter 466 in an action brought for treating, examining, or operating on a patient without his informed consent when:

(a)1. The action of the physician, osteopath, chiropractor, podiatrist, or dentist in obtaining the consent of the patient or another person authorized to give consent for the patient was in accordance with an accepted standard of medical practice among members of the medical profession with similar training and experience in the same or similar medical community; and

2. A reasonable individual, from the information provided by the physician, osteopath, chiropractor, podiatrist, or dentist, under the circumstances, would have a general understanding of the procedure, the medically acceptable alternative procedures or treatments, and the substantial risks and hazards inherent in the proposed treatment or procedures, which are recognized among other physicians, osteopaths, chiropractors, podiatrists, or dentists in the same or similar community who perform similar treatments or procedures; or

(b) The patient would reasonably, under all the surrounding circumstances, have undergone such treatment or procedure had he been advised by the physician, osteopath, chiropractor, podiatrist, or dentist in accordance with the provisions of paragraph (a).

(4)(a) A consent which is evidenced in writing and meets the requirements of subsection (3) shall, if validly signed by the patient or another authorized person, raise a rebuttable presumption of a valid consent.

(b) A valid signature is one which is given by a person who under all the surrounding circumstances is mentally and physically competent to give consent.

766.104. Pleading in medical negligence cases; claim for punitive damages

(1) No action shall be filed for personal injury or wrongful death arising out of medical negligence, whether in tort or

in contract, unless the attorney filing the action has made a reasonable investigation as permitted by the circumstances to determine that there are grounds for a good faith belief that there has been negligence in the care or treatment of the claimant. The complaint or initial pleading shall contain a certificate of counsel that such reasonable investigation gave rise to a good faith belief that grounds exist for an action against each named defendant. For purposes of this section, good faith may be shown to exist if the claimant or his counsel has received a written opinion, which shall not be subject to discovery by an opposing party, of an expert as defined in s. 768.45 that there appears to be evidence of medical negligence. If the court determines that such certificate of counsel was not made in good faith and that no justiciable issue was presented against a health care provider that fully cooperated in providing informal discovery, the court shall award attorney's fees and taxable costs against claimant's counsel, and shall submit the matter to The Florida Bar for disciplinary review of the attorney.

(2) Upon petition to the clerk of the court where the suit will be filed and payment to the clerk of a filing fee, not to exceed $25, established by the chief judge, an automatic 90-day extension of the statute of limitations shall be granted to allow the reasonable investigation required by subsection (1). This period shall be in addition to other tolling periods. No court order is required for the extension to be effective. The provisions of this subsection shall not be deemed to revive a cause of action on which the statute of limitations has run.

IDAHO CODE
Chapter 10

Medical Malpractice
6-1001. Hearing panel for prelitigation consideration of medical malpractice claims-Procedure.-

The Idaho state board of medicine, in alleged malpractice cases involving claims for damages against physicians and surgeons practicing in the state of Idaho or against licensed acute care general hospitals operating in the state of Idaho, is directed to cooperate in providing a hearing panel in the nature of a special civil grand jury and procedure for prelitigation consideration of personal injury and wrongful death claims for damages arising out of the provision of or alleged failure to provide hospital or medical care in the state of Idaho, which proceedings shall be informal and nonbinding, but nonetheless compulsory as a condition precedent to litigation. Proceedings conducted or maintained under the authority of this act shall at all times be confidential, privileged and immune from civil process and evidence of them or results, findings or determinations thereof shall be inadmissible in any civil or other action or proceeding by, against or between the parties thereto or any witness therein. Formal rules of evidence shall not apply and all such proceedings shall be expeditious and informal. [1976, ch. 278, § 2, p. 953.]

6-1002. Appointment and composition of hearing panel.-

The board of medicine shall provide for and appoint an appropriate panel or panels to accept and hear complaints of such negligence and damages, made by or on behalf of any patient who is an alleged victim of such negligence. Said panels, shall include one (1) person who is licensed to practice medicine in the state of Idaho. In cases involving claims against hospitals, one (1) additional member shall be a then serving administrator of a licensed acute care general hospital in the state of Idaho. One (1) additional member of each such panel shall be appointed by the commissioners of the Idaho state bar, which person shall be a resident lawyer licensed to practice law in the state of Idaho, and shall serve as chairman of the panel. The panelists so appointed shall select by unanimous decision a layman panelist who shall not be a lawyer, doctor or hospital employee but who shall be a responsible adult citizen of Idaho. All panelists shall serve under oath that they are without bias or conflict of interest as respects any matter under consideration. [1976, ch. 278, § 3, p. 953.]

6-1003. Informal proceedings.-

There shall be no record of such proceedings and all evidence, documents and exhibits shall, at the close thereof, be returned to the parties or witnesses from whom the same were secured. The hearing panel shall have the authority to issue subpoenas and to administer oaths; provided, the parties requesting the presentation of such proof shall provide the funds required to tender witness fees and mileage as provided in proceedings in district courts. Except upon special order of the panel, and for good cause shown demonstrating extraordinary circumstances, there shall be no discovery or perpetuation of testimony in said proceedings. [1976, ch. 278, § 4, p. 953.]

6-1004. Advisory decisions of panel.-

At the close of proceedings the panel, by majority and minority reports or by unanimous report, as the case may be, shall provide the parties its comments and observations with respect to the dispute, indicating whether the matter appears to be frivolous, meritorious or of any other particular description. If the panel is unanimous with respect to an amount of money in damages that in its opinion should fairly be offered or accepted in settlement, it may so advise the parties and affected insurers or third-party payors having subrogation, indemnity or provisions of law to the contrary and in the event there are no funds available, the political subdivision shall levy and collect a property tax, at the earliest time possible, in an amount necessary to pay a claim or judgment arising under the provisions of this act where the political subdivision has failed to purchase insurance or otherwise provide a comprehensive liability plan to cover a risk created under the provisions of this act. [1971, ch. 150, § 28, p. 743; am. 1976, ch. 310, § 8, p. 1069.]

6-1005. Tolling of limitation periods during pendency of proceedings.-

There shall be no judicial or other review or appeal of such matters. No party shall be obliged to comply with or otherwise [be] affected or prejudiced by the proposals, conclusions or suggestions of the panel or any member or segment thereof; however, in the interest of due consideration being given to such proceedings and in the interest of encouraging consideration of claims informally and without the necessity of litigation, the applicable statute of limitations shall be tolled and not be deemed to run during the time that such a claim is pending before such a panel and for thirty (30) days thereafter. [1976, ch. 278, § 6, p. 953.]

6-1006. Stay of other court proceedings in interest of hearing before panel.

During said thirty (30) day period neither party shall commence or prosecute litigation involving the issues submitted to the panel and the district or other courts having jurisdiction of any pending such claims shall stay proceedings in the interest of the conduct of such proceedings before the panel. [1976, ch. 278, § 7, p. 953.]

6-1007. Service of claim on accused provider of health care.-

At the commencement of such proceedings and reasonably in advance of any hearing or testimony, the accused provider of health care in all cases shall be served a true copy of the claim to be processed which claim shall set forth in writing and in general terms, when, where and under what circumstances the health care in question allegedly was improperly provided or withheld and the general and special damages attributed thereto. [1976, ch. 278, § 8, p. 953.]

6-1008. Confidentiality of proceedings.-

Neither party shall be entitled, except upon special order of the panel, to attend and participate in the proceedings which shall be confidential and closed to public observation at all times, except during the giving of his or her own testimony or presentation of argument of his or her position, whether by counsel or personally; nor shall there be cross-examination, rebuttal or other customary formalities of civil trials and court proceedings. The panel itself may, however, initiate requests for special or supplemental participation, in particular respects and of some or all parties; and communications between the panel and the parties, excepting only the parties' own testimony on the merits of the dispute, shall be fully disclosed to all other parties. [1976, ch. 278, § 9, p. 953.]

6-1009. Representation of parties by counsel.-

Parties may be represented by counsel in proceedings before such panels, though it shall not be required. [1976, ch. 278, § 10, p. 953.]

6-1010. No fees or compensation for panel members.-

There shall be no fees or compensation paid to, charged or collected by the panel members, who shall serve upon the sworn commitment that all related matters shall be held confidential and privileged. [1976, ch. 278, § 11, p. 953.]

6-1011. Limit on duration of proceedings-Panel's jurisdiction.-

There shall be no repeat or reopening of panel proceedings. In no case shall a panel retain jurisdiction of any such claim in excess of ninety (90) days from date of commencement of proceedings. If at the end of such ninety (90) day period the panel is unable to decide the issues before it, it shall summarily conclude the proceedings and the members may informally, by written communication, express to the parties their joint and several impressions and conclusions, if any, albeit the same may be tentative or based upon admittedly incomplete consideration; provided, by written agreement of all parties the jurisdiction of the panel, if it concurs therein, may be extended and the proceeding carried on for additional periods of thirty (30) days. [1976, ch. 278, § 12, p. 953.]

6-1012. Proof of community standard of health care practice in malpractice case.

In any case, claim or action for damages due to injury to or death of any person, brought against any physician and surgeon or other provider of health care, including, without limitation, any dentist, physicians' assistant, nurse practitioner, registered nurse, licensed practical nurse, nurse anesthetist, medical technologist, physical therapist, hospital or nursing home, or any person vicariously liable for the negligence of them or any of them, on account of the provision of or failure to provide health care or on account of any matter incidental or related thereto, such claimant or plaintiff must, as an essential part of his or her case in chief, affirmatively prove by direct expert testimony and by a preponderance of all the competent evidence, that such defendant then and there negligently failed to meet the applicable standard of health care practice of the community in which such care allegedly was or should have been provided, as such standard existed at the time and place of the alleged negligence of such physician and surgeon, hospital or other such health care provider and as such standard then and there existed with respect to the class of health care provider that such defendant then and there belonged to and in which capacity he, she or it was functioning. Such individual providers of health care shall be judged in such cases in comparison with similarly trained and qualified providers of the same class in the same community, taking into account his or her training, experience, and fields of medical specialization, if any. If there be no other like provider in the community and the standard of practice is therefore indeterminable, evidence of such standard in similar Idaho communities at said time may be considered. As used in this act, the term "community" refers to that geographical area ordinarily served by the licensed general hospital at or nearest to which such care was or allegedly should have been provided. [1976, ch. 288, § 2, p. 951.]

6-1013. Testimony of expert witness on community standard.-

The applicable standard of practice and such a defendant's failure to meet said standard must be established in such cases by such a plaintiff by testimony of one (1) or more knowledgeable, competent expert witnesses, and such expert testimony may only be admitted in evidence if the foundation therefor is first laid, establishing (a) that such an opinion is actually held be the expert witness, (b) that the said opinion can be testified to with reasonable medical certainty, and (c) that such expert witness possesses professional knowledge and expertise coupled with actual knowledge of the applicable said community standard to which his or her expert opinion testimony is addressed; provided, this section shall not be construed to prohibit or otherwise preclude a competent expert witness who resides elsewhere from adequately familiarizing himself with the standards and practices of (a particular) such area and thereafter giving opinion testimony in such a trial. [1976, ch. 277, § 3, p. 951.]

KANSAS STATUTES ANNOTATED

60-3405. Findings and purpose.

Substantial increases in costs of professional liability insurance for health care providers have created a crisis of availability and affordability. This situation poses a serious threat to the continued availability and quality of health care in Kansas. In the interest of the public health and welfare, new measures are required to assure that affordable professional liability insurance will be available to Kansas health care providers, to assure that injured parties receive adequate compensation for their injuries, and

60-3406. Definitions.

As used in K.S.A. 1986 Supp. 60-3406 through 60-3410 and amendments thereto:

(a) The words and phrases defined by K.S.A. 1986 Supp. 60-3401 and amendments thereto shall have the meanings provided by that section.

"Current economic loss" means costs of medical care and related benefits, lost wages and other economic losses incurred prior to the verdict.

(c) "Future economic loss" means costs of medical care and related benefits, lost wages, loss of earning capacity or other economic losses to be incurred after the verdict.

(d) "Medical care and related benefits" means reasonable expenses of necessary medical care, hospitalization and treatment required due to the negligent rendering of or failure to render professional services by the liable health care provider.

History: L. 1986, ch. 229, § 12; L. 1987, ch. 224, § 3; July 1.

60-3407. Limitations on compensatory damages.

(a) In any medical malpractice liability action:

(1) The total amount recoverable by each party from all defendants for all claims for noneconomic loss based on causes of action accruing before July 1, 1988, shall not exceed a sum total of $250,000; and

(2) subject to K.S.A. 1987 Supp. 60-3411, the total amount recoverable by each party from all defendants for all claims shall not exceed a sum total of $1,000,000.

(b) If a medical malpractice liability action is tried to a jury, the court shall not instruct the jury on the limitations imposed by this section or on the ability of the claimant to obtain supplemental benefits under K.S.A. 1987 Supp. 60-3411.

In a medical malpractice liability action, subject to apportionment of fault pursuant to K.S.A. 60-258a and amendments thereto:

(1) If the verdict results in an award for noneconomic loss which exceeds $250,000, the court shall enter judgment for $250,000 for all the party's claims for noneconomic loss.

(2) If the verdict results in an award for current economic loss which exceeds the difference between $1,000,000 and the amount awarded by the court for damages for noneconomic loss, the court shall enter judgment for an amount equal to such difference for all the party's claims for current economic loss.

(3) If the sum of the amounts awarded by the court for noneconomic loss and for current economic loss is $1,000,000 or more, no judgment shall be entered for future economic loss. If the sum of such amounts is less than $1,000,000 and the verdict results in an award for future economic loss which exceeds the difference between $1,000,000 and the sum of such amounts, the court shall enter judgment for the cost of an annuity contract which, to the greatest extent possible, will provide for the payment of benefits over the period of time specified in the verdict in the amount awarded by the verdict for future economic loss, the cost of such annuity not to exceed the difference between $1,000,000 and the sum of the amounts awarded by the court for noneconomic loss and current economic loss.

(d) The limitations on the amount of damages recoverable for noneconomic loss under this section shall be adjusted annually on July 1 by rule of the supreme court in proportion to the net change in the United States city average consumer price index for all urban consumers during the preceding 12 months.

(e) The provisions of this section shall not be construed to repeal or modify the limitation provided by K.S.A. 60-1903 and amendments thereto in wrongful death actions.

(f) The provisions of this section shall expire on July 1, 1993.

60-3412. Expert witnesses, qualifications.

In any medical malpractice liability action, as defined in K.S.A. 1985 Supp. 60-3401 and amendments thereto, in which the standard of care given by a practitioner of the healing arts is at issue, no person shall qualify as an expert witness on such issue unless at least 50% of such person's professional time within the two-year period preceding the incident giving rise to the action is devoted to actual clinical practice in the same profession in which the defendant is licensed.

History: L. 1986. ch. 229, § 17; July 1.

60-3413. Settlement conference.

(a) In any medical malpractice liability action, as defined by K.S.A. 1985 Supp. 60-3401 and amendments thereto, the court shall require a settlement conference to be held not less than 30 days before trial.

(b) The settlement conference shall be conducted by the trial judge or the trial judge's designee. The attorneys who will conduct the trial, all parties and all persons with authority to settle the claim shall attend the settlement conference unless excused by the court for good cause.

(c) Offers, admissions and statements made in conjunction with or during the settlement conference shall not be admissible at trial or in any subsequent action.

ILLINOIS ANNOTATED STATUTES

2-622. Healing art malpractice

§ 2-622. Healing art malpractice. (a) In any action, whether in tort, contract or otherwise, in which the plaintiff seeks damages for injuries or death by reason of medical, hospital, or other healing art malpractice, the plaintiff's attorney or the plaintiff, if the plaintiff is proceeding pro se, shall file an affidavit, attached to the original and all copies of the complaint, declaring one of the following:

1. That the affiant has consulted and reviewed the facts of the case with a health professional who the affiant reasonably believes is knowledgeable in the relevant issues involved in the particular action and who practices in the same specialty as the defendant if the defendant is a specialist; that the reviewing health professional has determined in a written report, after a review of the medical record and other relevant material involved in the particular action that there is a reasonable and meritorious cause for the filing of such action; and that the affiant has concluded on the basis of the reviewing health professional's review and consultation that there is a reasonable and meritorious cause for filing of such action. If the affidavit is filed as to a defendant who is a physician licensed to treat human ailments without the use of drugs or medicines and without operative surgery, a dentist, a podiatrist, or a psychologist, the written report must be from a health professional licensed in the same profession, with the same class of license, as the defendant. For affidavits filed as to all other defendants, the written report must be from a physician licensed to practice medicine in all its branches. In

either event, the affidavit must identify the profession of the reviewing health professional. A copy of the written report, clearly identifying the plaintiff and the reasons for the reviewing health professional's determination that a reasonable and meritorious cause for the filing of the action exists, must be attached to the affidavit, but information which would identify the reviewing health professional may be deleted from the copy so attached.

2. That the affiant was unable to obtain a consultation required by paragraph 1 because a statute of limitations would impair the action and the consultation required could not be obtained before the expiration of the statute of limitations. If an affidavit is executed pursuant to this paragraph, the certificate and written report required by paragraph 1 shall be filed within 90 days after the filing of the complaint. The defendant shall be excused from answering or otherwise pleading until 30 days after being served with a certificate required by paragraph 1.

3. That a request has been made by the plaintiff or his attorney for examination and copying of records pursuant to Part 20 of Article VIII of this Code and the party required to comply under those Sections has failed to produce such records within 60 days of the receipt of the request. If an affidavit is executed pursuant to this paragraph, the certificate and written report required by paragraph 1 shall be filed within 90 days following receipt of the requested records. All defendants except those whose failure to comply with Part 20 of Article VIII of this Code is the basis for an affidavit under this paragraph shall be excused from answering or otherwise pleading until 30 days after being served with the certificate required by paragraph 1.

(b) Where a certificate and written report are required pursuant to this Section a separate certificate and written report shall be filed as to each defendant who has been named in the complaint and shall be filed as to each defendant named at a later time.

(c) Where the plaintiff intends to rely on the doctrine of "es ipsa loquitur", as defined by Section 2-1113 of this Code, the certificate and written report must state that, in the opinion of the reviewing health professional, negligence has occurred in the course of medical treatment. The affiant shall certify upon filing of the complaint that he is relying on the doctrine of "res ipsa loquitur".

HAWAII
[CHAPTER 671]
MEDICAL TORTS

PART I. GENERAL PROVISIONS

§671-1 Definitions.

As used in this chapter:

(1) "Health care provider" means a physician or surgeon licensed under chapter 453, a physician or a physician and surgeon licensed under chapter 460, a health care facility as defined in section 323D-2, and the employees of any of them. Health care provider shall not mean any nursing institution or nursing service conducted by and for those who rely upon treatment by spiritual means though prayer alone, or employees of such institution or service.

(2) "Medical tort" means professional negligence, the rendering of professional service without informed consent, or an error or omission in professional practice, by a health

care provider, which proximately causes death, injury, or other damage to a patient.

§671-2 Attorney's contingent fees arrangements.

(a) In any action for medical tort in which the plaintiff's attorney and the plaintiff agree that the attorney is to be paid a fee only if the plaintiff recovers damages, payment to the attorney shall be limited to a reasonable amount as approved by a court of competent jurisdiction.

(b) If the plaintiff recovers damages as a result of settlement or arbitration award without the initiation of court action, the plaintiff's attorney shall submit the amount of the plaintiff's attorney's fee to the circuit court which would have had jurisdiction of the action or the circuit court of the circuit in which the plaintiff resides for approval.

(c) If the plaintiff recovers damages as a result of settlement, arbitration award or judgment after court action has been initiated, the plaintiff's attorney shall submit the amount of the plaintiff's attorney's fee to the court having jurisdiction of the action.

(d) Upon receiving a submission for approval of attorney's fees, the court shall approve the fee or so much thereof as it finds to be reasonable. [L 1976, c. 219, pt of §2; am L 1977, c 167, §3; am imp L 1984, c 90, §1]

§671-3 Informed consent; board of medical examiners standards.

(a) The board of medical examiners, insofar as practicable, shall establish standards for health care providers to follow in giving information to a patient, or to a patient's guardian if the patient is not competent to give an informed consent, to insure that the patient's consent to treatment is an informed consent. The standards may include the substantive content of the information to be given, the manner in which the information is to be given by the health care provider and the manner in which consent is to be given by the patient or the patient's guardian.

(b) If the standards established by the board of medical examiners include provisions which are designed to reasonably inform a patient, or a patient's guardian, of:

(1) The condition being treated;

(2) The nature and character of the proposed treatment or surgical procedure;

(3) The anticipated results;

(4) The recognized possible alternative forms of treatment; and

(5) The recognized serious possible risks, complications, and anticipated benefits involved in the treatment or surgical procedure, and in the recognized possible alternative forms of treatment, including nontreatment,then the standards shall be admissible as evidence of the standard of care required of the health care providers.

(c) On or before January 1, 1984, the board of medical examiners shall establish standards for health care providers to follow in giving information to a patient or a patient's guardian, to ensure that the patient's consent to the performance of a mastectomy is an informed consent. The standards shall include the substantive content of the information to be given, the manner in which the information is to be given by the health care provider and the manner in which consent is to be given by the patient or the patient's guardian. The substantive content of the information to be given shall include information on the recognized alternative forms of treatment.

(d) Nothing in this section shall require informed consent from a patient or a patient's guardian when emergency treatment or emergency surgical procedure is rendered by a health care provider and the obtaining of consent is not reasonably feasible under the circumstances without adversely affecting the condition of the patient's health.

§671-4 "Ad damnum" clause prohibited.

(a) No complaint, counterclaim, or cross-claim in an action for medical tort shall specify the amount of damages prayed for but shall contain a prayer for general relief, including a statement that the amount of damages is within the minimum jurisdictional limits of the court in which the action is brought.

(b) In any such medical tort action, the party against whom the complaint, counterclaim, or cross-claim is made may at any time request a statement setting forth the nature and amount of the damages sought. The request shall be served upon the complainant, counterclaimant, or crossclaimant who shall serve a responsive statement as to the damages within fifteen days thereafter. In the event a response is not served, the requesting party may petition the court with notice to the other parties, to order the appropriate party to serve a responsive statement.

(c) If no request is made for a statement setting forth the nature and amount of damages sought, the complainant, counterclaimant, or crossclaimant, as the case may be, shall give notice to the other of the amount of special and general damages sought to be recovered, either before a default may be taken, or in the event an answer is filed, at least sixty days prior to the date set for trial. [L 1976, c 219, pt of §2; am L 1980, c 232, §36]

§671-5 Reporting and reviewing medical tort claims.

(a) Every self-insured health care provider, and every insurer providing professional liability insurance for a health care provider, shall report to the insurance commissioner the following information about any medical tort claim, known to the self-insured health care provider or insurer, that has been settled, arbitrated, or adjudicated to final judgment within ten working days following such disposition:

(1) The name and last known business and residential addresses of each plaintiff or claimant, whether or not each recovered anything;

(2) The name and last known business and residential addresses of each health care provider who was claimed or alleged to have committed a medical tort, whether or not each was a named defendant and whether or not any recovery was had against each;

(3) The name of the court in which any medical tort action, or any part thereof, was filed and the docket number;

(4) A brief description or summary of the facts upon which each claim was based, including the date of occurrence;

(5) The name and last known business and residential addresses of each attorney for any party to the settlement, arbitration, or adjudication, and

identification of the party represented by each attorney;

(6) Funds expended for defense and plaintiff costs;

(7) The date and amount of settlement, arbitration award, or judgment in any matter subject to this subsection; and

(8) Actual dollar amount of award received by the injured party.

(b) The insurance commissioner shall forward the name of every health care provider, except a hospital or physician licensed under chapter 453 or an osteopathic physician and surgeon licensed under chapter 460, against whom a settlement is made, an arbitration award is made, or judgment is rendered to the appropriate board of professional registration and examination for review of the fitness of the health care provider to practice the health care provider's profession. The insurance commissioner shall forward the entire report under subsection (a) to the department of commerce and consumer affairs if the person against whom settlement or arbitration award is made or judgment rendered is a physician licensed under chapter 453 or an osteopathic physician and surgeon licensed under chapter 460.

(c) A failure on the part of any self-insured health care provider to report as requested by this section shall be grounds for disciplinary action by the board of medical examiners, board of osteopathic examiners, or the state health planning agency, as applicable. A violation by an insurer shall be grounds for suspension of its certificate of authority. [L 1976, c 219, pt of º2; am L 1983, c

SELECTED STATE STATUTES

PART II. MEDICAL CLAIM CONCILIATION

§67111 Medical claim conciliation panels; composition, selection, compensation.

(a) There are established medical claim conciliation panels which shall review and render findings and advisory opinions on the issues of liability and damages in medical tort claims against health care providers.

(b) A medical claim conciliation panel shall be formed for each claim filed pursuant to section 671-12 and after each panel renders its decision or the claim is otherwise disposed of it shall be disbanded. Each medical claim conciliation panel shall consist of one chairperson selected from among persons who are familiar with and experienced in the personal injury claims settlement process, one attorney licensed to practice in the courts of the State and experienced in trial practice, and one physician or surgeon licensed to practice under chapter 453 or chapter 460. The chairperson shall be appointed by the chief justice of the supreme court of Hawaii. The attorney shall be appointed by the chairperson from a list of not less than thirty-five attorneys experienced in trial practice submitted annually by the supreme court. The physician or surgeon shall be appointed by the chairperson from a list of not less than thirty-five physicians or surgeons licensed under chapter 453 submitted annually by the board of medical examiners or from a list of not less than eight physicians or physicians and surgeons licensed under chapter 460 submitted annually by the board of osteopathic examiners.

The chairperson shall preside at the meetings of the panel. The chairperson and all panel members shall be compensated at the rate of $100 per claim handled which will become payable when the decision of the panel is submitted and shall be paid allowances for travel and living expenses which may be incurred as a result of the performance of their duties on the panel. Such costs shall be paid by the department of commerce and consumer affairs.

The office and meeting space, secretarial and clerical assistance, office equipment, and office supplies for the panel shall be furnished by the department.

The board of medical examiners and board of osteopathic examiners shall each prepare a list of physicians, surgeons, or physicians and surgeons, as the case may be, along with their respective specialties who shall then be considered consultants to the panel in their respective fields. Panel members may consult with other legal, medical, and insurance specialists. Any consultant called by the panel to appear before the panel shall be paid an allowance for travel and living expenses which may be incurred as a result of such person's appearance before the panel. Such costs shall be paid by the department.

[§671-12] Review by panel required; notice; presentation of claims.

Effective July 1, 1976, any person or the person's representative claiming that a medical tort has been committed shall submit the claim to the medical claim conciliation panel before a suit based on the claim may be commenced in any court of this State. Claims shall be submitted to the medical claim conciliation panel orally or in writing on forms provided by the panel. If the claim is presented orally, the panel shall reduce the claim to writing. The claimant shall set forth facts upon which the claim is based and shall include the names of all parties against whom the claim is or may be made who are then known to the claimant. Within five business days thereafter the panel shall give notice of the claim, by certified mail, to all health care providers and others who are or may be parties to the claim and shall furnish copies of written claims to such persons. Such notice shall set forth a date, not more than twenty days after mailing the notice, within which any health care provider against whom a claim is made may file a written response to the claim, and a date and time, not less than five days following the last date for filing a response, for a hearing of the panel. Such notice shall describe the nature and purpose of the panel's proceedings and shall designate the place of the meeting. The times originally set forth in the notice may be enlarged by the chairperson, on due notice to all parties, for good cause.

§671-13 Medical claim conciliation panel hearing; fact-finding; evidence; voluntary settlement.

Every claim of a medical tort shall be heard by the medical claim conciliation panel within thirty days after the last date for filing a response. No persons other than the panel, witnesses, and consultants called by the panel, and the persons listed in section 671-14 shall be present except with the permission of the chairperson. The panel may, in its discretion, conduct an inquiry of a party, witness, or consultant without the presence of any or all parties.

The hearing shall be informal. Chapters 91 and 92 shall not apply. The panel may require a stenographic record of all or part of its proceedings for the use of the panel, but such record shall not be made available to the parties. The panel may receive any oral or documentary evidence. Questioning of parties, witnesses, and consultants may be conducted by the panel, and the panel may, in its discretion, permit any party, or any counsel for a party to question other parties, witnesses, or consultants. The panel may designate who, among the parties, shall have the burden of going forward with the evidence with respect to such issues as it may consider, and unless otherwise designated by the panel, when medical and hospital records have been provided the claimant for the claimant's proper review, such burden shall initially rest with the claimant at the commencement of the hearing.

The panel shall have the power to require by subpoena the appearance and testimony of witnesses and the production of documentary evidence. When such subpoena power is utilized, notice shall be given to all parties. The testimony of witnesses may be taken either orally before the panel or by deposition. In cases of refusal to obey a subpoena issued by the panel, the panel may invoke the aid of any circuit court in the State, which may issue an order requiring compliance with the subpoena. Failure to obey such order may be punished by the court as a contempt thereof. Any member of the panel may sign subpoenas, administer oaths and affirmations, examine witnesses, and receive evidence. Notwithstanding such powers, the panel shall attempt to secure the voluntary appearance, testimony, and cooperation of parties, witnesses, and consultants without coercion.

At the hearing of the panel and in arriving at its opinion the panel shall consider, but not be limited to, statements or testimony of witnesses, hospital and medical records, nurses' notes, X-rays, and other records kept in the usual course of the practice of the health care provider without the necessity for other identification or authentication, statements of fact, or opinion on a subject contained in a published treatise, periodical, book, or pamphlet, or statements of experts without the necessity of the experts appearing at the hearing. The panel may upon the application of any party or upon its own decision appoint as a consultant, an impartial and qualified physician, surgeon, physician and surgeon, or other professional person or expert to testify before the panel or to conduct any necessary professional or expert examination of the claimant or relevant evidentiary matter and to report to or testify as a witness thereto. Such a consultant shall not be compensated or reimbursed except for travel and living expenses to be paid as provided in section 671-11. Discovery by the parties shall not be allowed.

During the hearing and at any time prior to the rendition of an advisory decision pursuant to section 671-15, the panel may encourage the parties to settle or otherwise dispose of the case voluntarily.

§671-14 Same; persons attending hearings of panel.

Unless excluded or excused by the panel, the following persons shall attend hearings before the panel:

(1) The party or parties making the claim;

(2) The health care provider or providers against whom the claim is made or representatives thereof, other than counsel, authorized to act for such health care provider or providers;

(3) Counsel for the parties, if any.

671-15 Same, decisions.

(a) Within thirty days after the completion of a hearing, the medical claim conciliation panel shall file a written advisory decision with the insurance commissioner who shall thereupon mail copies to all parties concerned, their counsel, and the representative of each health care provider's liability

APPENDIX A

insurance carrier authorized to act for such carrier, and the board of osteopathic examiners, as appropriate. The insurance commissioner also shall mail copies of the advisory decision to the department of commerce and consumer affairs, if the claim is against a physician or surgeon licensed under chapter 453 or an osteopathic physician and surgeon licensed under chapter 460. The panel shall decide the issue of liability and shall state its conclusions in substantially the following language: "We find the health care provider was actionably negligent in his or her care and treatment of the patient and we, therefore, find for the claimant"; or "We find the health care provider was not actionably negligent in his or her care and treatment of the patient and we, therefore, find for the health care provider".

After a finding of liability, the medical claim conciliation panel shall decide the amount of damages, if any, which should be awarded in the case. The decision as to damages shall include in simple, concise terms a division as to which portion of the damages recommended are attributable to economic losses and which to noneconomic losses; provided the panel may not recommend punitive damages.

(c) The decisions shall be signed by all members of the medical claim conciliation panel; provided that any member of the panel may file a written concurring or dissenting opinion.

(d) The advisory decision required by this section need not be filed if the claim is settled or otherwise disposed of before the decision is written or filed.

§671-16 Subsequent litigation; excluded evidence.

The claimant may institute litigation based upon the claim in an appropriate court only after a party to a medical claim conciliation panel hearing rejects the decision of the panel, or after the eighteen-month period under section 671-18 has expired.

No statement made in the course of the hearing of the medical claim conciliation panel shall be admissible in evidence either as an admission, to impeach the credibility of a witness, or for any other purpose in any trial of the action, provided that such statements may be admissible for the purpose of section 671-19, hereof. No decision, conclusion, finding, or recommendation of the medical claim conciliation panel on the issue of liability or on the issue of damages shall be admitted into evidence in any subsequent trial, nor shall any party to the medical claim conciliation panel hearing, or the counsel or other representative of such party, refer or comment thereon in an opening statement, an argument, or at any other time, to the court or jury, provided that such decision, conclusion, finding, or recommendation may be admissible for the purpose of section 671-19, hereof.

[§671-17] Immunity of panel members from liability.

No member of a medical claim conciliation panel shall be liable in damages for libel, slander, or other defamation of character of any party to medical claim conciliation panel proceeding for any action taken or any decision, conclusion, finding, or recommendation made by the member while acting within the member's capacity as a member of a medical claim conciliation panel under this Act. [L 1976, c 219, pt of §2; am imp L 1984, c 90, §1]

APPENDIX A

§671-18 Statute of limitations tolled.

The filing of the claim with the medical claim conciliation panel shall toll any applicable statute of limitations, and any such statute of limitations shall remain tolled until sixty days after the date the decision of the panel is mailed or delivered to the parties; provided that in no case shall the applicable statute of limitations be tolled for more than eighteen months. If a decision by the medical claim conciliation panel is not reached within eighteen months, the statute of limitations shall resume running and the party filing the claim may commence a suit based on the claim in any

(d) When the attorney intends to rely on the doctrine of failure to inform of the consequences of the procedure, the attorney shall certify upon the filing of the complaint that the reviewing health professional has, after reviewing the medical record and other relevant materials involved in the particular action, concluded that a reasonable health professional would have informed the patient of the consequences of the procedure.

(e) Allegations and denials in the affidavit, made without reasonable cause and found to be untrue, shall subject the party pleading them or his attorney, or both, to the payment of reasonable expenses, actually incurred by the other party by reason of the untrue pleading, together with reasonable attorney's fees to be summarily taxed by the court upon motion made within 30 days of the judgment or dismissal. In no event shall the award for attorneys' fees and expenses exceed those actually paid by the moving party, including the insurer, if any. In proceedings under this paragraph (e), the moving party shall have the right to depose and examine any and all reviewing health professionals who prepared reports used in conjunction with an affidavit required by this Section.

UTAH CODE ANNOTATED

78-14-1. Short title of act.

This act shall be known and may be cited as the "Utah Health Care Malpractice Act."

78-14-2. Legislative findings and declarations - Purpose of act.

The legislature finds and declares that the number of suits and claims for damages and the amount of judgments and settlements arising from health care has increased greatly in recent years. Because of these increases the insurance industry has substantially increased the cost of medical malpractice insurance. The effect of increased insurance premiums and increased claims is increased care cost, both through the health care providers passing the cost of premiums to the patient and through the provider's practicing defensive medicine because he views a patient as a potential adversary in a lawsuit. Further, certain health care providers are discouraged from continuing to provide services because of the high cost and possible unavailability of malpractice insurance.

In view of these recent trends and with the intention of alleviating the adverse effects which these trends are producing in the public's health care system, it is necessary to protect the public interest by enacting measures designed to encourage private insurance companies to continue to provide health-related malpractice insurance while at the same time establishing a mechanism to ensure the availability of insurance in the event that it becomes unavailable from private companies.

In enacting this act, it is the purpose of the legislature to provide a reasonable time in which actions may be commenced against health care providers while limiting that time to a specific period for which professional liability insurance premiums can be reasonably and accurately calculated; and to provide other procedural changes to expedite early evaluation and settlement of claims.

78-14-3. Definition of terms.

As used in this act:

(1)"Health care provider" includes any person, partnership, association, corporation, or other facility or institution who causes to be rendered or who renders health care or professional services as a hospital, physician, registered nurse, licensed practical nurse, nurse-midwife, dentist, dental hygienist, optometrist, clinical laboratory technologist, pharmacist, physical therapist, podiatrist, psychologist, chiropractic physician, naturopathic physician, osteopathic physician, osteopathic physician and surgeon, audiologist, speech pathologist, certified social worker, social service worker, social service aide, marriage and family counselor, or practitioner of obstetrics, and others rendering similar care and services relating to or arising out of the health needs of persons or groups of persons, and officers, employees, or agents of any of the above acting in the course and scope of their employment.

(2) "Malpractice action against a health care provider" means any action against a health care provider, whether in contract, tort, breach of warranty, wrongful death or otherwise, based upon alleged personal injuries relating to

or arising out of health care rendered or which should have been rendered by the health care provider.

78-14-4. Statute of limitations - Exceptions - Application.

(1) No malpractice action against a health care provider may be brought unless it is commenced within two years after the plaintiff or patient discovers, or through the use of reasonable diligence should have discovered the injury, whichever first occurs, but not to exceed four years after the date of the alleged act, omission, neglect or occurrence, except that:

(a) In an action where the allegation against the health care provider is that a foreign object has been wrongfully left within a patient's body, the claim shall be barred unless commenced within one year after the plaintiff or patient discovers, or through the use of reasonable diligence should have discovered, the existence of the foreign object wrongfully left in the patient's body, whichever first occurs; and

(b) In an action where it is alleged that a patient has been prevented from discovering misconduct on the part of a health care provider because the health care provider has affirmatively acted to fraudulently conceal the alleged misconduct, the claim shall be barred unless commenced within one year after the plaintiff or patient discovers, or through the use of reasonable diligence, should have discovered the fraudulent concealment, whichever first occurs.

(2) The provisions of this section shall apply to all persons, regardless of minority or other legal disability under § 78-12-36 or any other provision of the law, and shall apply retroactively to all persons, partnerships, associations and corporations and to all health care providers and to all

malpractice actions against health care providers based upon alleged personal injuries which occurred prior to the effective date of this act; provided, however, that any action which under former law could have been commenced after the effective date of this act may be commenced only within the unelapsed portion of time allowed under former law; but any action which under former law could have been commenced more than four years after the effective date of this act may be commenced only within four years after the effective date of this act.

78-14-4.5. Amount of award reduced by amounts of collateral sources available to plaintiff - No reduction where subrogation right exists-Collateral sources defined - Procedure to preserve subrogation rights - Evidence admissible - Exceptions.

(1) In all malpractice actions against health care providers as defined in Subsection 78-14-3(29) in which damages are awarded to compensate the plaintiff for losses sustained, the court shall reduce the amount of such award by the total of all amounts paid to the plaintiff from all collateral sources which are available to him; however, there shall be no reduction for collateral sources for which a subrogation right exists as provided in this section nor shall there be a reduction for any collateral payment not included in the award of damages. Upon a finding of liability and an awarding of damages by the trier of fact, the court shall receive evidence concerning the total amounts of collateral sources which have been paid to or for the benefit of the plaintiff or are otherwise available to him. The court shall also take testimony of any amount which has been paid, contributed, or forfeited by, or on behalf of the plaintiff or members of his immediate family to secure his right to any collateral source benefit which he is receiving as a result of his injury, and shall offset any reduction in the award by such amounts. No evidence shall be received and no

reduction made with respect to future collateral source benefits except as specified in Subsection (4).

(2) For purposes of this section "collateral source" means payments made to or for the benefit of the plaintiff for:

(a) medical expenses and disability payments payable under the United States Social Security Act, any federal, state, or local income disability act, or any other public program, except the federal programs which are required by law to seek subrogation;

(b) any health, sickness, or income disability insurance, automobile accident insurance that provides health benefits or income disability coverage, and any other similar insurance benefits, except life insurance benefits available to the plaintiff, whether purchased by the plaintiff or provided by others;

(c) any contract or agreement of any person, group, organization, partnership, or corporation to provide, pay for, or reimburse the costs of hospital, medical, dental, or other health care services, except benefits received as gifts, contributions, or assistance made gratuitously; and

(d) any contractual or voluntary wage continuation plan provided by employers or any other system intended to provide wages during a period disability.

(3) To preserve subrogation rights for amounts paid or received prior to settlement or judgment, a provider of collateral sources shall serve at least 30 days before settlement or trial of the action a written notice upon each health care provider against whom the malpractice action has been asserted. The written notice shall state the name

and address of the provider of collateral sources, the amount of collateral sources paid, the names and addresses of all persons who received payment, and the items and purposes for which payment has been made.

(4) Evidence is admissible of government programs that provide payments or benefits available in the future to or for the benefit of the plaintiff to the extent available irrespective of the recipient's ability to pay. Evidence of the likelihood or unlikelihood that such programs, payments, or benefits will be available in the future is also admissible. The trier of fact may consider such evidence in determining the amount of damages awarded to a plaintiff for future expenses.

(5) No provider of collateral sources is entitled to recover the amounts of such benefits from a health care provider, the plaintiff, or any other person or entity as reimbursement for collateral source payments made prior to settlement or judgment, including any payments made under Chapter 19, Title 26, except to the extent that subrogation rights to amounts paid prior to settlement or judgment are preserved as provided in this section. All policies of insurance providing benefits affected by this section are construed in accordance with this section.

78-14-5. Failure to obtain informed consent - Proof required of patient - Defenses - Consent to health care.

(1) When a person submits to health care rendered by a health care provider, it shall be presumed that what the health care provider did was either expressly or impliedly authorized to be done. For a patient to recover damages from a health care provider in an action based upon the provider's failure to obtain informed consent, the patient must prove the following:

(a) that a provider-patient relationship existed between the patient and health care provider; and

(b) the health care provider rendered health care to the patient; and

(c) the patient suffered personal injuries arising out of the health care rendered; and

(d) the health care rendered carried with it a substantial and significant risk of causing the patient serious harm; and

(e) the patient was not informed of the substantial and significant risk; and

(f) A reasonable, prudent person in the patient's position would not have consented to the health care rendered after having been fully informed as to all facts relevant to the decision to give consent. In determining what a reasonable, prudent person in the patient's position would do under the circumstances, the finder of fact shall use the viewpoint of the patient before health care was provided and before the occurrence of any personal injuries alleged to have arisen from said health care; and

(g) the unauthorized part of the health care rendered was the proximate cause of personal injuries suffered by the patient.

(2) It shall be a defense to any malpractice action against a health care provider based upon alleged failure to obtain informed consent if:

(a) the risk of the serious harm which the patient actually suffered was relatively minor; or

(b) the risk of serious harm to the patient from the health care provider was commonly known to the public; or

(c) the patient stated, prior to receiving the health care complained of, that he would accept the health care involved regardless of the risk; or that he did not want to be informed of the matters to which he would be entitled to be informed; or

(d) the health care provider, after considering all of the attendant facts and circumstances, used reasonable discretion as to the manner and extent to which risks were disclosed, if the health care provider reasonably believed that additional disclosures could be expected to have a substantial and adverse effect on the patient's condition; or

(e) the patient or his representative executed a written consent which sets forth the nature and purpose of the intended health care and which contains a declaration that the patient accepts the risk of substantial and serious harm, if any, in hopes of obtaining desired beneficial results of health care and which acknowledges that health care providers involved have explained his condition and the proposed health care in a satisfactory manner and that all questions asked about the health care and its attendant risks have been answered in a manner satisfactory to the patient or his representative; such written consent shall be a defense to an action against a health care provider based upon failure to obtain informed consent unless the patient proves that the person giving the consent lacked capacity to consent or shows by clear and convincing proof that the execution of the written consent was in-duced by the defendant's affirmative acts of fraudulent misrepresentation or fraudulent omission to state material facts.

(3) Nothing contained in this act shall be construed to prevent any person eighteen years of age or over from refusing to consent to health care for his own person upon personal or religious grounds.

(4) The following persons are authorized and empowered to consent to any health care not prohibited by law:

(a) any parent, whether an adult or a minor, for his minor child;

(b) any married person, for a spouse;

(c) any person temporarily standing in loco parentis, whether formally serving or not, for the minor under his care and any guardian for his ward;

(d) any person eighteen years of age or over for his or her parent who is unable by reason of age, physical or mental condition, to provide such consent;

(e) any patient eighteen years of age or over;

(f) any female regardless of age or marital status, when given connection with her pregnancy or childbirth;

(g) in the absence of a parent, any adult for his minor brother or sister; and

(h) in the absence of a parent, any grandparent for his minor grandchild.

(5) No person who in good faith consents or authorizes health care treatment or procedures for another as provided by this act shall be subject to civil lability.

78-14-6. Writing required as basis for liability for breach of guarantee, warranty, contract or assurance of result.

No liability shall be imposed upon any health care provider on the basis of an alleged breach of guarantee, warranty, contract or assurance of result to be obtained from any health care rendered unless the guarantee, warranty, contract or assurance is set forth in writing and signed by the health care provider or an authorized agent of the provider.

78-14-7. Ad damnum clause prohibited in complaint.

No dollar amount shall be specified in the prayer of a complaint filed in a malpractice action against a health care provider. The complaint shall merely pray for such damages as are reasonable in the premises.

78-14-7.1. Limitation of award of noneconomic damages in malpractice actions.

In a malpractice action against a health care provider, an injured plaintiff may recover noneconomic losses to compensate for pain, suffering, and inconvenience. In no case shall the amount of damages awarded for such noneconomic loss exceed $250,000. This limitation does not affect awards of punitive damages.

APPENDIX B

Peer Review

and

Malpractice Screening Panels

APPENDIX B
Peer Review and Malpractice Screening Panel

Connecticut General Statutes Annotated

38-19a. Peer review: Definitions; immunity; discovery permissible re proceedings

(a) For the purposes of this section:

(i) "Health care provider" means any person, corporation, facility or institution licensed by this state to provide health care or professional services, or an officer, employee or agent thereof acting in the course and scope of his employment.

(ii) "Peer review" means the procedure for evaluation by health care professionals of the quality and efficiency of services ordered or performed by other health care professionals, including practice analysis, inpatient hospital and extended care facility utilization review, medical audit, ambulatory care review and claims review.

(iii) "Professional society" includes medical, psychological, nursing, dental, naturopathic, osteopathic, optometric, pharmaceutical, chiropractic and podiatric organizations as well as individual practice associations as defined in Section 300e-1(5) of the Public Health Service Act, 42 U.S.C. 300e-1(5), as amended, having as members at least a majority of the eligible licentiates in the area or health care facility or agency served by the particular society.

(iv) "Medical review committee" shall include any committee of a state or local professional society or a committee of any health care institution established pursuant to written bylaws, and any utilization review committee established pursuant to Public Law 89-97, and a professional standards review organization or a state-wide professional standards review council, established pursuant to Public Law 92-603, engaging in peer review, to gather and review information relating to the care and treatment of patients for the purposes of (1) evaluating and improving the quality of health care rendered; (2) reducing morbidity or mortality; or (3) establishing and enforcing guidelines designed to keep within reasonable bounds the cost of health care. It shall also mean any hospital board or committee reviewing the professional qualifications or activities of its medical staff or applicants for admission thereto.

(b) There shall be no monetary liability on the part of, and no cause of action for damages shall arise against, any person who provides testimony, information, records, documents, reports, proceedings, minutes or conclusions to any hospital, hospital medical staff, professional society, medical or dental school, professional licensing board or medical review committee when such communication is intended to aid in the evaluation of the qualifications, fitness or character of a health care provider and does not represent as true any matter not reasonably believed to be true.

(c) There shall be no monetary liability on the part of, and no cause of action for damages shall arise against, any member of a medical review committee for any act or proceeding undertaken or performed within the scope of any such committee's functions provided that such member has taken action or made recommendations without malice and in the reasonable belief that the act or recommendation was warranted.

(d) The proceedings of a medical review committee conducting a peer review shall not be subject to discovery or introduction into evidence in any civil action for or against a health care provider arising out of the matters which are subject to evaluation and review by such committee, and no person who was in attendance at a meeting of such committee shall be permitted or required to testify in any such civil action as to the content of such proceedings; provided the provisions of this subsection shall not preclude (1) in any civil action, the use of any writing which was recorded independently of such proceedings; (2) in any civil action, the testimony of any person concerning the facts which formed the basis for the institution of such proceedings of which he had personal knowledge acquired independently of such proceedings; (3) in any health care provider proceedings concerning the termination or restriction of staff privileges, other than peer review, the use of data discussed or developed during peer review proceedings; or (4) in any civil action, disclosure of the fact that staff privileges were terminated or restricted, including the specific restrictions imposed, if any.

§ 38-19b. Malpractice screening panel established

There is established within the insurance department the "malpractice screening panel" which shall consist of members whose names shall be supplied by the Connecticut State Medical Society and the Connecticut Bar Association. This panel may be added to whenever the need arises by requesting further names from either the Connecticut State Medical Society or the Connecticut Bar Association. Members of the panel shall serve without compensation. The insurance commissioner may designate a member of his department to administer the operation of and maintain the records for such screening panel.

§ 38-19e Confidentiality of proceedings, records, findings and deliberations

All proceedings, records, findings and deliberations of a hearing panel shall be confidential and shall not be used in any other proceedings, or otherwise publicized, except as provided in this chapter, nor disclosed by any party, witness, counsel, panel member or other person, on penalty of being found in contempt of court. The manner in which a hearing panel and each member thereof deliberates, decides and votes on any matter submitted to it, including whether its final decision is unanimous or otherwise, shall not be disclosed or made public by any person, except as provided in this chapter.

§ 38-19f. Finding as to liability

At the conclusion of its hearing and deliberation, the panel shall make a finding as to liability only signed by all members and record the same with the insurance commissioner who shall forward a copy of the same to the parties. The finding, if unanimous, shall be admissible in evidence at any subsequent trial of the issues. The trier, whether court or jury, shall determine what if any weight should be afforded said finding. The finding shall speak for itself and no member of the panel shall be subject to subpoena or required to testify regarding the same. Any explanation of the finding or the panel shall be at the discretion of the trial judge.

APPENDIX C
Summary of State Statutes

APPENDIX C

SUMMARY OF STATE STATUTES: DISCOVERY AND ADMISSIBILITY OF MEDICAL RECORDS

ARIZONA
Ariz. Rev. Stat. Ann. §36-445.01:

All proceedings, records, and materials prepared in relation to committees that review the nature, quality, and necessity of care provided in a hospital and the preventability of complication and deaths occurring in a hospital, including all peer reviews of individual health care providers practicing in and applying to practice in hospitals, and the records of such reviews are confidential and not subject to discovery. Discovery is allowable in action by an individual health care provider against a hospital or staff arising from discipline of that health care provider, or refusal, termination, suspension, or limitation of his or her privileges.

CALIFORNIA
Cal. Evid Code §1157 (West 1985):

The proceedings and records of organized medical staff committees, the function of which is to evaluate and improve the quality of care rendered in a hospital, are not subject to discovery. No person in attendance at a committee meeting can be required to testify as to what transpired there. The probition relating to discovery does not apply to statements made by a person who attended such a committee meeting and who is a party to an action or proceeding, the subject of which was reviewed at the meeting, or to any person requesting staff privileges.

COLORADO
Colo. Rev. Stat. §12-43.5-102:

The records of peer review committees or other committees that perform similar review services are not subject to subpoena in any civil suit against a physician. The Colorado Stat.e Board of Medical examiners may obtain a summary of the findings, recommendations, and disposition of action taken by a review committee.

CONNECTICUT
Conn. Gen Stat. Ann. §38-19a (West):

Opinions of peer review, utilization review, medical audit, and similar committees are not subject to discovery and are not admissible into evidence in any civil action arising out of matters that are subject of committee evaluation and review.

DELAWARE
Del. Code Title 24 §1768:

Records and proceedings of hospital and nursing home quality review committees are confidential and not available for court subpoena or subject to discovery.

FLORIDA
Fla. Stat. Ann. §768.40 (West):

The records and proceedings of quality assurance and utilization review committees are not subject to discovery or admissible into evidence in any civil action against a health care provider arising out of matters that are subject of committee evaluation and review. Material otherwise available from original sources is not immune from discovery or use in civil actions.

GEORGIA
Ga. Code Ann. §88-3204:

Records and proceedings of committees, the function of which is to evaluate and improve quality of health care rendered by health care providers or to determine that services rendered were professionally indicated or that the cost of services was reasonable, are not subject to discovery or introduction into evidence against a provider of professional health care services arising out of matters that are the subject of evaluation and review. Information, documents, or records otherwise available from original sources are not immune from discovery or use in civil actions because they were presented to a committee.

APPENDIX C

HAWAII
Haw. Rev. Stat. §624-25.5:

Proceedings and records of peer review committees are not subject to discovery. This prohibition does not apply to the statements made by any person in attendance at a committee meeting who is a party to an action or proceeding, the subject of which was reviewed at such meeting, or to any person who has requested hospital staff privileges.

ILLINOIS
Ill. Ann. Stat. ch 110 §8-2101, 8-2102 (Smith-Hurd):

Information, interviews, reports, statements, or other data of patient care audit, medical care evaluation, utilization review, and similar committees are strictly confidential and not admissible. The claim of confidentiality cannot be invoked in any hospital proceeding concerning a physician's staff privileges or in a judicial review of such a proceeding.

INDIANA
Ind. Code Ann. §34-4-12.6-1, 43-4-12.6-2 (Burns):

Records of the determinations of or communications to a peer review are not subject to discovery or admissible into evidence. Information otherwise discoverable or admissible from original sources is not immune from discovery or use only because it was presented during committee hearings. Any professional health care provider who is under investigation has the right to see any records pertaining to his/her personal practice.

IOWA
Iowa Code Ann. §135.40, 135.42 (West):

Information, interviews, reports, statements, memos, and other data used by hospital staff committees in the course of any study, the aim of which is to reduce morbidity, are not to be used, offered , or received in evidence. This section does not affect the admissibility of a patient's primary medical or hospital records.

KANSAS
Kan. Stat. Ann. §65-177:

Opinions based on data collected in medical research studies conducted by the state health officer on the subject of reducing mortality and morbidity from maternal, perinatal and anesthetic causes are not admissible in any action in court. Statistics or tables resulting from such studies are admissible.

LOUISIANA
La. Rev. Stat. Ann. §447.7 (West):

The records and proceedings of any hospital committee, medical organization committee or extended care facility are no available for court subpoena.

APPENDIX C

MAINE
Me. Rev. Stat. Ann. title 32, §3296:

All proceedings and records of proceedings of mandatory medical staff review committees and hospital review committees are exempt from discovery without a showing of good cause.

MARYLAND
Md. Health Acc Code Ann. §14-601:

The proceedings, records, and files of a medical review committee are neither discoverable nor admissible into evidence in any civil action arising out of matters that are not subject of committee evaluation and review.

MASSACHUSETTS
Mass. Gen. Laws Ann. ch 231 §85N (West):

Members of professional committees are not liable in civil action except for bad faith or reckless decisions.

MICHIGAN
Mich. Stat. Ann. §14.57(23) (Callaghan):

All proceedings, reports, findings, and conclusions of review entitleies are confidential and shall not be discoverable or used as evidence in an action for personal injuries based upon malpractice, lack of informed consent, or negligence.

SUMMARY OF STATE STATUTES

MINNESOTA
Minn. Stat. Ann. §145, 61-65 (West):

Data and information of quality of assurance, mortality and morbidity, cost control, and similar committees are not subject to subpoena or discovery. The proceedings and records of these committees are not subject to discovery or introduction into evidence in any civil action against a health care professional arising out of matters that are subject of evaluation and review. Documents or records otherwise available from original sources are not immune simply because they were presented during the proceedings of a review organization.

MISSOURI
Mo. Stat. §537.035 (Vernon):

Members of medical review, peer review, utilization review, pharmacy review, and similar committees are not liable in any damages to any person subject to the actions of such committees unless the actions were malicious or insupportable.

MONTANA
Mont. Code Ann. §5016-201, 50-16-201, 50-16-205:

Data of tissue committees and committees that function to assist in the training, supervision, and discipline of health care professional is confidential and not admissible in evidence in any judicial proceeding. This statute does not affect the admissibility of records dealing with a patient's hospital care and treatment.

NEBRASKA
Neb. Rev. Stat. §71-2046, 71-2048:

The proceedings, records, minutes, reports, and communications of medical staff committees and utilization review committees are not subject to discovery except upon court order after a showing of good cause arising from extraordinary circumstances. This statute does not preclude or affect discovery of a production of evidence relating to the hospitalization or treatment of any patient in ordinary course of hospitalization of such patient.

NEVADA
Nev. Rev. Stat. §49.265:

The proceedings and records medical review committees and organized medical staff committees responsible for evaluating and improving the quality of care rendered in hospitals are not subject to discovery. This statute does not apply to any statement made by an applicant for hospital staff privileges; nor does it apply to any statement made by an applicant for hospital staff privileges; nor does it apply to any statement made by a person in attendance at a committee meeting who is a party to an action or proceeding, the subject of which is reviewed at such meeting.

SUMMARY OF STATE STATUTES

NEW JERSEY
N.J. Stat. Ann. §2A.8A-22.8 (West):

Information and data secured by utilization review committees may not be revealed or disclosed in any manner or in any circumstances except to (1) a patient's attending physician, (2) the chief administrative officer of a hospital that such committees serve, (3) the medical executive committee of a hospital, (4) representatives of governmental agencies in the performance of their duties, or (5) insurance companies, under certain conditions.

NEW YORK
N.Y. Educ Law §6527 (West):

Proceedings and utilization review records, quality control, and similar committees are not subject to disclosure. This exemption from disclosure does not apply to statements made by any person in attendance at a committee meeting who is a party to an action or proceeding, the subject of which was reviewed at the meeting.

NORTH CAROLINA
N.C. Gen. Stat. §131E-95:

Members of committees formed for the purpose of evaluating the quality, cost, or necessity of hospitalization or health care services are not subject to liability in civil actions, except in cases of malice or fraud. In a civil action against a provider of professional health services, records and materials either considered or produced by a committee are not subject to discovery or introduction into evidence where the action arises out of matters that are the subject of evaluation and review by the committee.

OHIO
Ohio Rev. Code Ann. §2305.25, 2305.1 (Anderson):

Proceedings and records of tissue, utilization review, peer review, and similar committees are confidential and are not subject to discovery or introduction into evidence in any civil action arising our of matters that are subject of evaluation and review. Information, documents, or records otherwise available from original sources are not immune from discovery or use merely because they were presented during committee meetings.

OREGON
Or. Rev. Stat. §41.675:

All data of tissue, utilization review and similar committees are confidential and are not admissible in evidence in any judicial proceeding. This statute does not affect the admissibility in evidence of records dealing with a patient's hospital care and treatment.

SUMMARY OF STATE STATUTES

PENNSYLVANIA
Pa. Stat. Ann. title 63, §§425.2, 425.4 (Purdon):

The proceedings and records of peer review, utilization review, medical audit, claims review, and similar committees are not subject to discovery or introduction into evidence in any civil action against a professional health provider arising out of matters that are the subject of evaluation and review. Information, documents, or records otherwise available from original sources are not immune simply because they were presented during committee proceedings.

SOUTH CAROLINA
S.C. Code Ann. §§40-71-10, 40-71-20 (Law Co-op):

All proceedings and all data and information acquired by committees formed to maintain professional standards are not subject to discovery, subpoena, or introduction into evidence except upon appeal from a committee's action. Information, documents, and records that are otherwise available from original sources are not immune from discovery or use simply because they were presented before a committee.

TENNESSEE
Tenn. Code Ann. §63-6-219:

All information of health care quality assurance, cost containment, and utilization review committees is not available for subpoena or discovery. But material that is otherwise available from original sources is not protected merely because it was presented before a committee.

TEXAS
Tex. Rev. Civ. Stat. Ann. article 4447d (Vernon):

The records and proceedings of committees formed to reduce morbidity or mortality or to identify persons who may be in need of immunization are confidential and are not available for court subpoena. This statute does not apply to records kept by a hospital in the regular course of its business.

UTAH
Utah Code Ann. §§26-25-1, 26-25-3:

All information, interviews, reports, statements, memoranda, and other data of committees, the function of which is to reduce morbidity or mortality or to evaluate and improve the quality of hospital and medical care, are privileged and are not to be used or received into evidence in any legal proceeding.

VERMONT
Vt. Stat. Ann. Title 26, §§1441, 1443:

The proceedings, reports, and records of committees formed to evaluate and improve the quality of health care rendered by providers of health care services or to determine whether their cost was reasonable are neither discoverable nor admissible in any civil action against a health care provider arising out of matters that are the subject of evaluation and review. Information, reports, or documents otherwise available from original sources are not immune from discovery or use in civil actions simply because they were presented before a committee.

VIRGINIA
Va. Code Ann. §§8.01-581.16, 8.01-581.17:

The proceedings, records, minutes, reports, and oral and written communications of cost control, utilization review, quality control, peer review, and similar committees are privileged and are not discoverable except under court order after a showing of good cause arising from extraordinary circumstances. This statute does not immunize hospital records kept with respect to any patient in the ordinary course of the business of operating a hospital.

WASHINGTON
Wash. Rev. Code Ann. §4.24.250:

Written records of committees formed to evaluate the competence and qualifications of members of the health care profession are not subject to subpoena or discovery in any civil action, except actions arising out of a committee's recommendations.

APPENDIX C

WISCONSIN
Wis. Stat Ann. §146.38:

Records of organizations formed to review and evaluate the services of health care providers may not be used in civil actions against health care providers or facilities. Information, documents, and records are not to be construed as immune from discovery or use in civil actions merely because they were presented to a committee. Information can be released for medical and other specified purposes as long as the names of patients are withheld.